TECHNOLOGY AND THE GENDERING OF MUSIC EDUCATION

To my parents Margaret and George
with love

Technology and the Gendering of Music Education

VICTORIA ARMSTRONG
St Mary's University College, Twickenham, UK

ASHGATE

Published by
Ashgate Publishing Limited
Wey Court East
Union Road
Farnham
Surrey, GU9 7PT
England

Ashgate Publishing Company
Suite 420
101 Cherry Street
Burlington
VT 05401-4405
USA

www.ashgate.com

British Library Cataloguing in Publication Data
Armstrong, Victoria.
  Technology and the gendering of music education.
  1. Computer composition – Study and teaching – Sex differences.
  2. Sex differences in education. 3. Music and technology.
  4. Technology and women. 5. Gender identity in music.
  I. Title
  781.3'4'081–dc22

Library of Congress Cataloging-in-Publication Data
Armstrong, Victoria.
  Technology and the gendering of music education / Victoria Armstrong.
      p. cm.
  Includes bibliographical references and index.
  ISBN 978-1-4094-1784-2 (hardcover : alk. paper)—ISBN 978-1-4094-3413-9
  (ebook) 1. Computer music—Instruction and study—Great Britain.
  2. Music—Instruction and study—Technological innovations.
  3. Sex differences in education—Great Britain. 4. Music and technology.
  I. Title.
  MT3.G7A76 2011
  781.3'4071—dc22

2011010616

ISBN 9781409417842 (hbk)
ISBN 9781409434139 (ebk)

UNIVERSITIES AT MEDWAY
25 APR 2012
DRILL HALL LIBRARY

Printed and bound in Great Britain by the
MPG Books Group, UK.

Contents

Acknowledgements

I would like to express my sincere thanks to those whose help and support has sustained me throughout the writing of this book. Firstly, I would like to express my gratitude to Lucy Green. She has been an inspiration not only for her challenging intellectual insights but for her kind and invaluable support and guidance over the years. I would like to acknowledge friends and colleagues who offered encouragement and invaluable feedback at different stages of the book including Diana Adams, Sally Barnes, Barbara Bradby, Nick Breeze, Ruth Craggs, Nicola Dibben, Marina Gall, Diana Leonard and Rosamund Sutherland. In addition, I would like to thank John Morgan for bringing to my attention the work of social geographers interested in critically examining educational spaces and to Ross Purves for his helpful remarks during the embryonic stages of Chapter 4 regarding the gendering of music software.

I have also been lucky enough to benefit from the professional expertise and sensible advice about the writing process from Isobel Armstrong and John Burrow both of whom helped me to move forward when inspiration waned. I would like to pay particular tribute to the late Diana Wynne-Jones who showed me great kindness over the years. A much loved writer who, even in the final stages of her illness, continued to write with such passion and beauty. The memory of her great love of language, ideas and the world of the imagination remain strong and I will hold on to this memory when, no doubt, inspiration will again wax and wane in future writing projects!

Thanks must also go to the editorial team at Ashgate, particularly Heidi Bishop and Ann Allen for their helpful editorial advice.

Heartfelt thanks to the pupils and teachers who participated in this research, for their interest in the project and for their generosity and kindness in making me feel welcome in their classrooms. Conversations with them were often moving, always thought-provoking and tremendously enjoyable. I hope I have done justice to their creativity and passion for music.

I would also like to extend my thanks to the GCSE and A level pupils at the secondary school I worked in during the late 1990s. They know who they are but unfortunately cannot be personally identified as I have written about their experiences in other academic papers. Their generous insights into their compositional processes sparked off my curiosity about gender and composition, which provided the inspiration for this book.

Inevitably, I turn now to my family. This book is dedicated to my parents, whose love and encouragement have sustained me throughout my various endeavours and whose belief in me has never wavered. I owe them so much.

Finally, as is customary but with a sense of extreme good fortune, I acknowledge the love and support of my husband, Tom Armstrong. As a professional composer, musician and music educator, over the years he has listened patiently to my ideas and arguments from first 'hunches' to fully fledged arguments, and his helpful musical insights through our many long conversations have made an important contribution to the ideas presented in the book, particularly with regards to the compositional process. He has stimulated, encouraged and challenged me every step of the way, and his support has been unwavering throughout.

Chapter 1

Introduction

This book is about the construction of gendered identities in the music technology classroom. It explores how gendered discourses around music composition and technology are constructed and how young composers position themselves within these discursive frameworks. Since 1987, music composition has become a key element of the National Curriculum (which sets national standards for what students should learn) for music in England and Wales, and increasingly music technology has become central to this activity in primary and secondary schools. The contemporary music classroom is not only becoming increasingly technologized but, as some would argue (Finney and Burnard, 2007), 'revolutionized' by the use of Information and Communication Technology (ICT) with ever greater investment in computers and compositional software.

Ostensibly, the benefits of this increased technologization might appear unequivocal but, as Pitts (2000) points out, the level of debate within music education has been minimal in comparison to its level of use. Much of the current literature in music education focuses on pedagogical issues, educational outcomes and the role of ICT in raising standards (Busen-Smith, 1999; Mills and Murray, 2000; Savage and Challis, 2001; Pitts and Kwami, 2002). This literature appears to assume that, with sufficient access to both the computer and the requisite knowledge of music software, all pupils will benefit from engaging with music technologies when composing and will wish to do so. This deterministic trend in the literature ignores the socially constructed nature of computers and computer use, which renders the current rhetoric lauding the 'democratizing' potential of computers somewhat inadequate and naive. While there have been a number of studies exploring the gendered implications of music technology in the classroom (Comber et al., 1993; Caputo, 1994; Colley et al., 1997; Pegley, 2000; Armstrong, 2008), paradoxically, at a time when music technology courses[1] are proliferating in schools and universities, the paucity of current academic studies in the field is surprising given that music technology is less likely to attract girls but is said to be of positive benefit for male pupils (Comber et al., 1993; Colley et al., 1997; Green, 1997; Byrne and MacDonald, 2002).

This uncritical rhetoric is encapsulated in the assertion that 'the most significant implications for the application of the software in the secondary classroom lie

---

[1]   Boehm (2007) charts the landscape of music technology in British Universities, examining the pedagogic and institutional differences between the 351 degrees that currently come under the category 'music technology', and some of the tensions inherent in the interdisciplinary model that typifies how music technology degrees are taught.

in its inclusivity' (Mellor, 2008: 469), a claim which fails to acknowledge the ways in which technologies become gendered, in their material use, their symbolic meanings and their ideological function despite the well-documented differential in girls' and boys' computer use within other educational settings (Kiesler et al., 1985; Bromley and Apple, 1998; Clegg, 2001; Stepulevage, 2001; Colley and Comber, 2003) whereby males are often viewed as more 'expert' users than their female counterparts and as a result have greater influence in shaping the culture of computer use within the classroom:

> The dominant discourse in computing is shaped by social practices which have institutionalized the power of experts, mostly male, to define what counts as computing in education ... these ideologies in turn shape the climate which women have to negotiate. (Clegg, 2001: 308)

Clegg's observation is an important one and yet is largely overlooked in the recent push for increased use of technology as a key remediation strategy in subjects where boys are perceived to be underachieving (Warren, 2003).[2] The apparent appeal of technology is linked to boys' out-of-school interests in computer-based activities and is believed to encourage their greater educational participation and increase motivation (BECTA, 2008), the aim being to raise standards while making learning fun, invoking what Renold and Allan (2006) call the discourse of 'enjoyment'. Of concern here is how little attention is paid to how this technological focus will affect girls' performance, a situation increasingly common when developing pedagogical strategies to improve boys' performance (Younger and Warrington, 2008; Skelton and Francis, 2009).

Within the music classroom similar arguments have been employed in an effort to encourage more boys to take up school music (Savage, 2007), making it more attractive for those who come from a rock and pop background (Byrne and Macdonald, 2002), as girls are more likely than boys to possess traditional instrument skills. A further imperative emanates from the argument that recent 'gender research in music education has been increasingly dominated by feminist theory', and has resulted in girls' musical experiences and needs being privileged over their male counterparts (Harrison, 2010: 40). Studies show that such a rationale is indeed having the desired effect: increased use of music technology is encouraging more boys to take up general music Advanced (A) level, in 2008 slightly more boys than girls took the General Certificate of Secondary Education

---

[2]   For an overview of some of the key debates around gender and educational achievement see Epstein et al (1998) and Francis and Skelton (2005). Archer and Francis (2007) examine the intersections between gender, class and 'race' in their discussion of educational achievement while Skelton and Francis (2009) offer a critical feminist reading of the discourse of boys' underachievement.

(GCSE)[3] music examination, and boys were found to be five times more likely to be entered for technology A level (Ofsted, 2009). Recent statistics also show that there is a significant gender differential in the number of UK university undergraduates studying music, with women making up only 41.5 per cent of music undergraduates (Farrar, 2007). As the technological focus has been increasing since the late 1990s, what we could be witnessing is a shift from a traditionally 'feminine' subject to a subject that has increasingly masculine connotations.

Consequently, this technicist framing of music education (Mansfield, 2005) raises important issues about gender and inclusion that much of the current music education literature fails to address. There appears to be an assumption that music technologies are unencumbered with the 'old baggage' of gendered social relations, but it is important to remember that these technologies are used and developed within existing social spaces that are always already delineated along gender lines (Green, 1997) and which are likely to reproduce and reinforce existing gender hierarchies. As Faulkner (2001: 79) has pointed out, nearly two decades of government initiatives to get more girls and women into the traditionally male dominated areas of science and technology have been unsuccessful because there has been a failure 'to critically examine the ways in which technology … gets gendered in the eyes of would-be technologists'. This book is therefore fuelled by the concern that, by failing to engage with the sociocultural contexts of technological use, we will continue to present an unproblematic picture of technology in the music classroom, one which fails to accurately reflect the social practices and experiences of young male and female composers, and overlooks the social reproductive effects of the classroom vis-à-vis gender relations.

The gender–technology relationship

Williams asserts that '[A] technology is always, in a full sense, social'. The take-up and use of technologies are shaped by the gendered social relations of the world into which they enter and, as such, are bound up with issues of power, authority and forms of control, a relationship that it is 'necessarily in complex and variable connection with other social relations and institutions' (Williams, 1981: 227). Questions about who developed the technology, for what purposes, in whose interests and with what consequences draw our attention to the powerful social structures at play in technological spheres. While it would be unwise to imply that technologies are inherently masculine, I would suggest that both the continuing *material* and *symbolic* associations of technology with men and masculinity contribute to the perception of women as less able and less interested in all things technological. As Turkle (1984) notes, it is not that computers contain an inherent

---

[3]   The General Certificate of Secondary Education (GCSE) examination is taken in the final year of compulsory schooling at the age of 16. The two year Advanced (A) level provides a standard entry qualification into undergraduate study at University .

gender bias but it is the culture surrounding them which produces socialized expectations of male and female behaviours and attitudes towards computers. This argument frames the position I have taken throughout the book, which is concerned with interrogating the continuing articulation between masculinity and technology as one of the ways that gendered social relations come to be embedded in the social processes of technology. This framework defies the kind of simplistic treatments in which technology is presented as either a product of male interests or as a 'neutral tool' because it obliges us 'to view gender as an integral part of the social shaping of technology' (Faulkner, 2001: 90).

Although individuals employ different strategies for 'doing' gender, Francis (2000: 16) asserts there is one 'notional' masculinity and one 'notional' femininity constructed as oppositional, leading her to interpret 'the various "kinds" of masculinity and femininity ... as the various ways in which men/boys attempt to achieve masculinity and femininity. In other words there are different strategies for constructing oneself as masculine or feminine, rather than different types of masculinity or femininity.' This focus on *strategies* reflects my own conceptualization of identity as I am interested in how practices seek to define and map the production of the gendered subject. As Walkerdine (1998: 165) points out, 'practices create subjectivities ... those practices read materiality in a particular way: they tell stories which are profoundly oppressive'. As gender relations are a process in which 'masculinity and femininity are descriptions of categories that are continually constructed, negotiated and renegotiated' (Ormrod, 1994: 36) this allows us to 'investigate the mundane processes by which these categories are constituted' (Ormrod, 1994: 37). Consequently, I am interested in the ways in which boys and girls construct themselves as masculine and feminine in the music classroom within the discursive frameworks available to them.

Examining these discursive frameworks helps uncover 'that what we take to be the "truth" is not an eternal and unchangeable fact, but a construction brought about in the dialectical interplay between the historical processes of society's reproduction and the individual's formation of identity' (Green, 1997: 4). Discourse 'constructs, defines and produces objects of knowledge in an intelligible way' (Barker, 2000: 56) that appears to 'make sense' but serves to exclude other definitions thereby limiting the interpretive possibilities open to those positioned within these discourses. Discourses shape how we understand and act within the world and comes to represent 'truths' for those who have the power to construct such definitions and for those who are oppressed by them. As Francis observes:

> gender difference is socially produced and often limiting to both sexes. Moreover, this social construction of gender difference holds important consequences in terms of power, because in the dichotomous construction of gender, power is located in the male, and the female is subjugated ... The main point about discourses is that they carry power in their ability to position things and people as negative or positive, powerless or powerful. (Francis, 2000: 19)

However, the concept of discourse is not a passive construct, and it is this active construction that holds the possibility for change ever mindful that these subject positions may not be voluntary because of the political and social structures through which dominant femininities and masculinities are produced (Laurie, 1999 cited in Reay, 2001). Accordingly, when looking at the construction of identity we must take into account that the active processes in the production of individual and collective identities always occur within socially given conditions which include structures of power and social relations (Epstein and Johnson, 1998). Francis's observation that 'it does not necessarily follow that, just because people can choose which discourses to draw on, they do so in any completely consistent or coherent way' (2001: 75) is particularly relevant. It helps to focus our attention on who has the power to construct gendered discourses in the music technology classroom and how the performance of gender by both teachers and pupils is enacted in ways that either comply with or resist these powerful discourses.

Gendering composition, gendering technology

In the following I aim to illustrate the connections between women's musical compositions and their contributions to technology, both of which have been denigrated and positioned in opposition to the contributions of their male counterparts. Teasing out these parallels begins to highlight the theoretical perspective I have adopted throughout this book drawing on the fields of gender and music, and feminist science and technology studies (STS) to aid in my discussion. Both music composition and technology have been historically and socially constructed along similar lines, with their focus on technical knowledge, expertise, rationality and mental logic, attributes which supposedly characterize men and masculinity. A prolific period of feminist writing about music in the late 1980s and 1990s drew attention to some critical issues regarding the subordination and marginalization of women's music (LePage, 1980; Neuls-Bates, 1982; Bowers and Tick, 1987; Shepherd, 1987; McClary, 1991; Pendle, 1991; Citron, 1993; Solie, 1993; Cook and Tsou, 1994; Dunn and Jones, 1994; Jezic, 1994; Halstead, 1997).[4] Presenting powerful arguments about how gender ideologies are constructed and maintained through musical practices, these texts act as a long awaited corrective to the hitherto unchallenged supremacy of hegemonic masculinity that underpins discourses about music. As Green (1997: 5) notes, although some of the dominant discourses on music may be accepted as 'common sense' by many, 'others are subservient, or articulate alternative perspectives'. As discourses jostle and compete for dominance, there will always be the possibility for resistance, and this offers the potential for new discourses and new meanings to be produced that challenge existing discourses about gender and music.

---

[4]   Dibben (2002) offers a succinct overview of the key issues surrounding gender and music.

Within Western thought, the dualisms that construct the oppositional male/ female, mind/body, reason/emotion, culture/nature splits reproduce a gendered discourse that polarizes masculinity and femininity, and we construct musical experiences and meanings through this gendered lens. Green (1997) argues that there are two distinct aspects of musical meaning, the first of which lies within the organization and conventional interrelationships of the musical materials. These *inherent* musical meanings are part of the listener's learnt understandings of how musical materials relate to each other.[5] In addition, the listener also brings other experiences to bear on the music, such as their own cultural and social position or perception of the performer (such as appropriate mode of dress or their gender, for example). These *delineated* meanings operate dialectically with music's inherent meanings and, whether consciously or not, our listening experiences are never devoid of these meanings. Green argues that when we see a woman performing or listen to the work of a female composer her femininity becomes part of the music's delineations. However, whereas the female singer affirms her femininity through the perceived alliance of her sound with her body, devoid of the need to control or employ external forms of technology, the female composer challenges patriarchal notions of femininity. In order to create the technical object (music), the composer must have technical knowledge of instruments and harmony in order to create the musical work, as well as an understanding of both technology and compositional technique, leading Green to suggest that composition becomes a 'metaphorical display of the mind' (1997: 84). Therefore, 'part of the musical delineation includes the notion of the mind behind the music, and part of the notion of mind is that it is masculine' (1997: 88). The woman composer's 'metaphorical, delineated display of mind conflicts with her natural submission to her body' (1997: 88). A similar point is made by Citron (1993), who also argues that the male appropriation of creativity relies on this ideology that links creativity to the mental, although this may appear contrary to how we perceive the arts as they are understood as dealing with emotions; emotions grounded in the natural body and thus 'feminized'. As such, 'feminine emotion' must be supplanted by the 'rational' masculine mind; rational knowledge that transcends and subordinates 'feminine' emotions. Even though the male creative genius is allowed to take on these 'feminized' attributes, when applied to females these attributes are not accorded the same status (Battersby, 1989).

In similar ways, feminist STS has also highlighted the gendered discourse that underpins discussions about masculinity, science and technology, which Murray (1993) suggests is not surprising given masculinity's attempt to define itself by its monopoly over the control of reason, logic and objectivity. He further argues that technology is the core domain of socially constructed masculinity and acts

---

[5]   In her book, *Music, informal learning and the school: a new classroom pedagogy*, Green (2008) has replaced the term 'inherent meaning' with 'inter-sonic meaning'. While theoretically the same, the latter apparently more clearly encapsulates the ways in which the sonic or musical properties of a piece of music are heard by the listener.

as a 'boundary marker'; that is, if it is technological it must be masculine, and therefore plays an important role in constructing male identity. It has been argued that technology is never neutral but is always already actively imbued with power of one sort or another; an important consideration when we note that women are more traditionally users and consumers than designers or producers of technology (Berg, 1994). Thus, Game and Pringle (1984: 36) claim that men are able to 'represent the power of the machine as theirs and experience themselves as having "technical" expertise ... the machine symbolizes masculinity and enables them to live out fantasies about power and domination which in turn reproduce this connection'. They suggest that it is necessary for men to maintain the 'mystification of machines' in order to preserve not only male jobs but the symbolic association of men's work with skill.

Traditionally, music, and particularly some realms of music performance, was viewed as a feminine domain, although composition is historically associated with masculinity. Consequently, with the introduction of technology, also traditionally perceived as a masculine domain, another layer of symbolic masculinity is added to an already gendered music classroom, where teachers perceive boys as having greater 'natural' ability for both technology (Comber et al., 1993; Caputo, 1994; Colley et al., 1997) and composition (Green, 1997). Gendered ideologies within Western art music continue to inform notions of what constitutes a composer, and this composer is invariably male. Consequently, just as technology and technological use are constructed around their symbolic associations with masculinity, so has composition maintained symbolic associations with masculinity through very similar processes. As such, the continued gendering of technology and composition presents a much more complicated picture of music technologies and their use in the classroom than is often acknowledged.

Defining technology

Definitions of 'technology' have shifted considerably over time and, as Street (1992) notes, defining a term depends on teasing out shared understandings of the way in which it is used. It is not my intention to provide an historical overview of its different meanings, but it is worth briefly setting out how the term is used throughout the book.[6] Early conceptualizations of technology focused on hardware, a machine or tool developed to carry out a designated activity or achieve a particular purpose but contemporary understandings commonly employed in cultural studies and STS offer a broader definition. In addition to the concept of technology as a tool or artefact, it can also be viewed as a system requiring appropriate knowledge and skill but is also constituted in social processes affecting and reflecting types of social relations. This conceptualization includes cultural values and ideologies (Murphie and Potts, 2003) whereby technology is seen to depend 'upon the way it

---

[6]   For a brief overview of the historical shifts that have occurred around the definitions of technology see Street (1992) and Murphie and Potts (2003).

is integrated into the understanding individuals and groups have of themselves and the world they inhabit' (Street, 1992: 12). As such, technology can be thought of as a 'system' or 'network' that involves people and organizations (Street, 1992), a system embedded in social relations created and enacted by people. This highlights the fundamental role of *human agency*: the piece of technological machinery does not work on its own; it may have been designed or programmed to carry out a particular task but that task has a human hand behind it. While much of the current literature refers to music information and communication technology (ICT), I would suggest this produces a tendency to only focus on the instrumental 'tool-like' aspects of technology. Unfortunately, this can result in ICT being problematically 'considered merely as neutral tools for learning' (Buckingham, 2007: viii) and yet this definition continues to be employed in educational policy documents where ICT is viewed as a tool for learning, reduced to a set of skills requiring appropriate knowledge and understanding. Consequently, the social nature of computer use is completely lost in this definition. By uncritically referring to educational technology as merely a tool (Bromley and Apple, 1998) we lose sight of the fact that not only are tools themselves never neutral, but technologies are systems which involve complex language structures and social structures (Hatfield, 2000). We surely cannot talk about educational technologies as mere 'things' devoid of any form of sociocultural context, because this fails to capture the complexities of the social 'embeddedness' of technology in which human choices are involved in producing the dynamics and direction of technological development (May, 2003). Ultimately, I hold on to Wajcman's (2004: 34) notion that 'technology is a socio-technical product, patterned by the conditions of its creation and use'. Therefore, throughout the book, I will adopt the term *music technology* rather than music ICT (and will refer to ICT only when other texts make explicit use of this term) as it better represents how the use of digital music technology (such as computers, minidisk players, and music notation software or sequencing packages) requires and produces knowledge, while also reflecting the cultures and values of the social context in which it is used.

Introducing the research

The findings presented in this book are based on an empirical study carried out in four secondary schools over a concentrated six-month period from January to June 2003. It explored the compositional experiences of pupils aged fifteen to eighteen, all of whom were studying for either GCSE or A level music, as music composition within this age group is normally carried out individually (rather than in groups) for examination purposes. The research is located within a qualitative paradigm in that it is concerned with observing forms of interaction and types of talk within the classroom, and understanding pupils' expressed views on their compositional experiences.

It is important to highlight that the study examined the compositional *process* rather than the actual product. By exploring *how* the music is produced rather than *what* is produced allowed me to better understand how boys and girls work with music technology during the various stages of the process (from the initial musical idea through the developmental, exploratory stage). By observing them composing and interviewing them about their compositional strategies, I was able to incorporate their own perspectives, which are central to this book, into this account:

> Studying the process focuses our attention on the creator's perspective; his or her thoughts, acts and understanding of the activity become the basis of their description. In contrast, studying the product implies a shift in focus where the music is separated from its creator and is regarded as an independent object seen and analysed from the perspective of the observer … [F]ocusing upon the process instead of the completed product is to say that it is not the music itself that is the focus but the practice of musical creation. (Folkestad, 1998: 6)

Had I undertaken an analysis of the musical work it would have been necessary to develop an analytical framework that could take into account the fact that many of the pieces written by these young composers are often subject to teachers' interventions. While teachers are expected to document their contribution in the selection of initial ideas (AQA, 2008), teachers can be significantly involved in this part of the process and may set the parameters of the work in terms of musical idea or style. They may also involve themselves in the development of pupils' work to the point where the teacher's idea has a tendency to overwhelm those of the pupils, as the following interview extract from an A level pupil in my study demonstrates:

> *Carolyn:* Um, I started with a very good idea for the song but then I hit a hard wall sort of thing. I hit a barrier and it's quite hard for me to get over that and that was the point at which his [*the teacher's*] influence on the piece came in because he was getting quite frustrated that I wasn't getting on with this piece and I was finding it quite difficult getting on with the piece so he just went 'Well, do this, do that, think about the instruments coming in there' and giving me these ideas and I just went with them because I couldn't think of anything else to do. Um, and I think that meant that it came out sort of with quite a lot of his ideas. (A Level girl, Crossways Independent)

My interest lies in understanding the gendered nature of teachers' musical interventions in their pupils' compositions because, as the research progressed, it became evident that these interventions were differently configured depending on whether the pupil was male or female (an issue explored further in Chapter 5). Ultimately, I am interested in the meanings adolescents attribute to the role music technology plays in their compositional processes rather than developing a systematic framework for analysing the composition itself.

Background and context of participating schools

The study was carried out in four secondary schools: one was located in inner London, two in outer London boroughs and one in the south east of England. They were selected on the basis of the following criteria gleaned from reports from the Office for Standards in Education (Ofsted), which inspects and regulates educational provision in England, and the schools' websites. The participating schools had to have access to and use music technology for composition teaching, and they had to be co-educational and offer both GCSE and A level music. Seven schools were initially identified as possibilities but, for the purposes of my study, it was also important that the participating schools represented a range of music technology provision and history rather than be schools with similar characteristics; the gendered make-up of the music department was also a consideration, as I wished to include one school with an all-male teaching staff and one with an all-female teaching staff. This resulted in four participating schools, hereafter referred to as Old Tech Grammar, New Tech Comprehensive, Crossways Independent and Arts College.

Below are brief vignettes of each school, which provide contextual information including the percentage of pupils taking formal instrumental lessons, the range of extracurricular music activities offered, levels of attainment at GCSE and the gender make-up of the music department. It should also be noted that, with the exception of Crossways Independent, the schools were predominantly white UK heritage and this is reflected in the music classes I observed.[7] Furthermore, apart from Arts College, all heads of department were male. The school roll includes sixth formers (studying for their A levels) and numbers are rounded up to prevent ease of identification and ensure anonymity. Throughout the book pseudonyms are used for names of the schools, pupils and teachers who took part, matching cultural names where appropriate.

Old Tech Grammar: school roll 1300

This selective grammar school is situated in an outer London borough in an area characterized as well above average in terms of socioeconomic status. Eighty per cent of pupils are of white heritage. The school consistently achieves significantly

---

[7]   Examining ethnicity as is relates to music education goes beyond the remit of this book but see Harris (2006) for a discussion on music education and Muslim pupils and Philpott's chapter entitled 'Ethnicity and music education' in Wright (ed) (2010).

higher than average GCSE results.[8] The music department consisted of two male teachers and one female teacher. Music technology provision and music resources were extremely high as the school had recently built a separate centre in which all music teaching took place. The main music room comprised sixteen electronic keyboards and headphones, and there was a small recording studio plus a modern dedicated music technology suite with twelve MIDI[9] keyboards and computers, together with minidisk players and CD-writing facilities. In addition, there was a third teaching room with a piano and hi-fi, plus three practice rooms, one housing a drum-kit. Around 15 per cent of pupils received instrumental and singing tuition at school with additional tuition provided at the local borough music school. The numerous extracurricular music groups included an orchestra, madrigal group, jazz band and choir.

New Tech Comprehensive: school roll 1600

This school is a non-selective comprehensive situated in the south east of England, with a large proportion of pupils coming from socially and economically advantaged homes. The pupils were predominantly of white heritage with a small number of pupils from other black and minority-ethnic backgrounds. It too has a higher than average pass rate at GCSE. The department consisted of two male teachers and one female teacher. There were two main teaching rooms. In the main room there were three music stations with MIDI keyboards and PCs, and there was a fourth MIDI keyboard and PC in a separate practice room next door (a computer–pupil ratio of 1:3). The second teaching room contained twelve electronic keyboards with headphones. There were also five practice rooms, one of which contained a drum kit. Some 9 per cent of the school population received formal instrumental tuition, and at A level 84 per cent of pupils had taken instrumental or singing exams. The school placed a strong emphasis on extracurricular music with a range of activities including a choir, orchestra, jazz band, guitar ensemble and woodwind ensemble. Over a third of pupils studying for GCSE and A level also played in orchestras and bands outside of school.

Crossways Independent: school roll 850

This school is an academically selective independent school situated in inner London, with around 50 per cent of its intake coming from black and minority-ethnic backgrounds. Figures for the GCSE examinations indicate that it has far exceeded the government's targets. The music department consisted of two male teachers. Numbers taking music in the school were exceptionally small. The

---

[8]   The Government's 'floor target' for 2011 is set at thirty per cent of pupils achieving at least 5 A*-C GCSEs including English and Mathematics in all secondary schools.

[9]   MIDI stands for 'Musical Instrument Digital Interface which 'allows electronic instruments to communicate by using a standardised set of commands' (Hugill, 2008: 84).

provision of a music technology room was a recent addition to the department, and consisted of three computers, two of which were connected to a keyboard (a computer–pupil ratio of 1:2). Music was very much a minority subject in this school, evidenced by the low numbers opting to take this subject at GCSE and A level. Around 20 per cent of pupils had formal instrumental and/or singing lessons and there were numerous extracurricular activities to which the large group of peripatetic teaching staff contributed, ranging from close harmony groups to rock bands.

Arts College: school roll 1200

This school is a non-selective comprehensive located in an outer London borough which had been awarded specialist schools status in the performing arts. Parents are characterized as 'below average' in terms of socioeconomic status, with only around 6 per cent of pupils from black and ethnic minority backgrounds. Although the school did not achieve as high a percentage of GCSEs as the other schools in the study, the pass rate was still some 15 per cent above government targets. The music department consisted of three female teachers. The dedicated music technology room contained a hi-fi system and sixteen workstations consisting of a MIDI keyboard connected to a computer (a computer–pupil ratio of 1:1) arranged around the outside of the room facing the wall, with a square of tables and chairs in the centre of the room for general teaching. In addition, there were three practice rooms and two music teaching rooms. Out of the whole school population, 13 per cent of pupils were taking formal instrumental or singing lessons, with more girls than boys taking formal exams. More than 50 per cent of the male pupils taking GCSE music played either drums or guitar. There was little extracurricular music provision.

The study

As the book is concerned with the sociocultural context in which composition takes place I adopted a multi-method approach combining classroom observation, pupil questionnaires, and individual teacher and pupil interviews. This meant I was able to consider the gendered interactions around technological use and expertise through firsthand experience of the classroom, which could then be followed up in more detail during the interviews. Observation notes enabled me to check inferences made from one data source against others, as what people say they do and what they actually do is not always identical. This is not to suggest that they deliberately set out to mislead the researcher, but often different data sources will offer contrasting perspectives on the same phenomenon (Heath et al., 2009). However, where possible discrepancies arise, adopting multiple methods helps make sense of such anomalies, which I have tried to capture in the presentation of the data and discussion.

While adhering to what Heath et al. (2009) call 'ethical absolutes' regarding confidentiality and anonymity, carrying out gender research raised the issue of what to tell pupils and teachers regarding the focus of the study. Addressing similar concerns faced by Francis (2000) in her study of gender and ethnicity in the secondary classroom, I was concerned that if I provided too much detail about the gendered aspect of my work, this knowledge might affect the participants' interactions, making them feeling self-conscious and lead to possible monitoring of their behaviours in the classroom. During the introductory presentation given to each class involved in the study, I informed the pupils that I was interested in their compositional processes using music technology, and that I would like to talk to them about their likes and dislikes and confidence levels with regard to music technology and composition, what they felt they were particularly good at, their preference for particular types of music software, and the amount of time they spent using music technology at home and at school. I concluded by outlining what taking part would entail, how long I planned to visit the school and that interviews would take place outside of lesson time. However, I did not make explicit reference to gender, although I mentioned to the teachers that questions about gender would be a key element of the interviews. This required the use of 'situated ethics' (Heath et al., 2009: 22) where researchers have to make ethical judgements based on the particular situation in which they find themselves. Ultimately, I had to balance this ethical concern against the aims of the study, and I believe my decision was appropriate under the circumstances as the integrity of the data might have been jeopardized had a full explication of the research been volunteered. This was not an easy decision to make, as one of the central aims of feminist approaches to research is that of 'empowerment', a term used to describe 'an enabling power to do something rather than a power over someone' (Humm, 1995: 78). I concluded that the types of questions I asked during the interviews were not harmful in any way to the participants' well-being, and this ultimately informed my decision to proceed on this basis. I provided numerous opportunities to 'opt out', and reminded participants at the start of their interview that they could withdraw at any time or 'pass' on any questions they did not wish to answer (although none took up this offer).

Often young people may feel compelled to make themselves understood in adult-centred terms (although this is not to imply that adult respondents do not also monitor and filter their responses accordingly) and, because of this requirement to make sense for adults, the interview may not necessarily be an empowering occasion for young people (Alldred, 1998). Nevertheless, follow-up comments made by pupils to their teachers and sometimes by the pupils themselves included remarks such as 'it was really good to be able to talk about my work properly' or 'I really felt I was being listened to', which were heartening. Participants' willingness to engage in conversation formally and informally and the thoughtful responses they offered when discussing their composing suggest that their participation in the study was largely a positive experience and that none experienced any harm owing to my decision.

Before providing a more detailed account of my methods, Table 1.1 gives information about the gender breakdown and number of pupils and teachers participating in the study.

Table 1.1 Gender and number of pupils and teachers in each class observed

School	GCSE pupils	A level pupils	Teachers
Old Tech Grammar	11 (7 boys, 4 girls)	8 (5 boys, 3 girls)	3 (2 male, 1 female)
New Tech Comprehensive	21 (15 boys, 6 girls)	13 (3 boys, 10 girls)	3 (2 male, 1 female)
Crossways Independent	6 (4 boys, 2 girls)	4 (2 boys, 2 girls)	2 (2 male)
Arts College	14 (5 boys, 9 girls)	7 (2 boys, 5 girls)	3 (3 female)
TOTAL	52 (31 boys, 21 girls)	32 (12 boys, 20 girls)	11 (6 male, 5 female)

Methods

At the beginning of the project, questionnaires were administered to all the pupils in the GCSE and A level classes observed. In comparison to the problem of administering questionnaires when the researcher is absent, which is likely to minimize the number of completed returns, having pupils complete the questionnaires during my first visit (and any pupils not in attendance during the first visit were asked to complete it on a subsequent visit) resulted in 81 completed forms.[10] The questionnaire was used to build up a picture of each school's musical culture and elicited information about the pupil's gender, age and level of study. It comprised four sections: sections A and B provided information regarding age, gender and course of study, the instruments they played and to what level, section C asked about their musical activities both at school and outside of school, and section D focused on music technology such as the types of software and hardware they use and how much time they spent using it. In addition, pupils were asked to nominate a 'technological expert': the person they felt was most competent at using music technology in their class. A final section asked pupils to indicate if they were happy to be interviewed (all but three agreed), which necessitated including their names on the form. However, as teachers were never given access to the completed forms, because they were administered and collected by me during lessons, this was not an issue with regards to pupil confidentiality. The questionnaire also aided in the purposive sampling of pupils, and, to ensure balance, selection was based on a pupil's typicality or atypicality: for example,

---

[10]   Three (from New Tech Comprehensive) were discounted as two of the respondents replicated each other's answers verbatim, and one was defaced.

where a pupil appeared to be representative of the class (based on the music department's profile) or seemed unusual for some reason (for example, a pupil who had been unanimously nominated as the 'technological expert').

The aim of the classroom observations was two-fold: firstly, they were used to develop an understanding of how and in what ways social interactions produce gendered classroom cultures around music technology, and secondly to observe the pupils composing. I undertook three lesson observations of one GCSE and one A level class in each school (six in each school, making twenty-four observations in total) each lasting from fifty minutes to one hour and forty minutes. Field notes were taken throughout each lesson unless I was in a situation where it seemed inappropriate to do so, such as sitting in a practice room observing a pupil composing; such close proximity would have made note-taking rather intrusive, but these were written up as soon as possible after the event, usually in the following break time or lunch hour.

Even when the researcher is not supposedly part of the interaction, knowledge of her presence may have a significant effect (Hammersley and Atkinson, 1983). Therefore, while carrying out the observations, I was aware that my presence might cause some sense of disruption to the setting. While recognizing that it is never possible to measure the extent to which my presence was impacting on the pupils and teachers, I would suggest that, by my attending lunch-time and after-school concerts and rehearsals, and often organizing my observations so that I could spend a half day or even whole day in the department, participants gradually got used to my presence, occasionally coming over to chat if I was milling around in the music room or technology suite during a lunch break. The extremely generous level of freedom afforded me during my visits also led to numerous spontaneous conversations with teachers; therefore, when content was appropriate to the study, this is noted.

Given the mobile nature of the music classroom, I also had to adopt a reflexive approach that acknowledged my part in classroom interactions when it occurred. The mobility of the music classroom often means that researchers have to make choices about exactly what to observe; this impacts on what the observer sees and the role the researcher is compelled to adopt in these different spaces. For example, at Arts College and Old Tech Grammar this was reasonably straightforward as pupils were all taught together in the music technology suite. However, the layout at New Tech Comprehensive and Crossways Independent meant pupils were scattered around the department in practice rooms, the main teaching room or where the computers were located. This was exacerbated at Crossways Independent where, due to the small numbers of students taking music, observing composing invariably meant sitting in a practice room with pupils working independently. Despite my aim to be a nonparticipant observer this role was virtually impossible to maintain. Consequently, as my role fluctuated from participant to nonparticipant observer according to the school and activity taking place, where relevant I make explicit reference to this in the ensuing discussion. During my introduction at each school, pupils invariably asked if I had taught music or, in one case, did I 'know anything about music?' to both of which I replied in the affirmative. I was happy to provide this information as I believe it helped establish my credibility but, when observing a pupil composing, this also meant I was likely to be placed in the role of a substitute teacher, being asked to play additional parts on the piano when they were composing or to give advice on a point of harmony, for example. I only intervened when called upon to do so, but to refuse help in these situations was likely to have produced a difficult and possibility damaging relationship with the pupils who may have then perceived me as unfriendly and unhelpful. Having taught pupils of this age for some time I was well aware that trust and approachability are important elements in establishing good working relationships with young people, and I wanted them to feel comfortable around me as I would become a regular visitor in the school. I was also mindful that this might result in a different relationship with the pupils from that which would normally have been expected with other classroom visitors such as school inspectors or PGCE tutors observing trainees on teaching practice; in these situations the relationship between pupil and observer operates within accepted codes of behavior, such as using a formal mode of address (such as 'Sir' or 'Miss'). Adopting formal modes of address are likely to exacerbate the power relations that exist between adults and young people in schools. I was keen to lessen this in my interactions with the pupils but, despite my best efforts, this was not always easy to achieve. Although I introduced myself by my first name to the pupils, teachers generally referred to me as 'Miss' while in the classroom, which meant that the pupils also referred to me in the same way, which accorded me the (unwanted) status of an adult 'guest' which could not be completely alleviated.

Finally, I carried out individual semi-structured interviews of about thirty minutes' duration with two boys and two girls from each GCSE and A level class (eight from each school; thirty-two in total). There were six rather than eight teachers interviewed, as the same teacher taught GCSE and A level at Arts College and Crossways Independent; these interviews usually lasted around an hour. The purpose of the individual teachers' interviews was to illuminate the department's use and development of music technology, technology's role in the compositional process, and their perceptions of gender in this context. All interviews were recorded and transcribed in full. The pupil interviews explored four main themes: confidence, learning about music technology and what they liked and disliked about technology; their perceptions of the teachers' and other pupils' level of technological expertise; generating and developing a musical idea (the compositional stimulus); and, finally, the role of technology in the compositional process. With a semi-structured format, respondents were free to elaborate on areas that they found of particular relevance or interest, and by asking open questions such as 'can you describe how you went about composing one of your recent pieces', I hoped to avoid the common problem of respondents providing researchers with what they would consider the 'right answer'. In contrast to the findings of Francis (2000: 28) none of the participating pupils came across as 'awkward' or 'monosyllabic' (around a third of the interviews lasted longer than the allocated thirty minutes, and I suspect my heightened presence around the department prior to the interviews taking place helped in this regard.

When interpreting young people's accounts of their practices it is helpful to note Lemke's (1995: 138) observation that 'fabulous fictions' construct childhood, and have been invented about 'the effects of normal hormonal processes of maturation on their judgement', and this was a construction of my young participants that I strived to counter. Throughout, I aimed to treat my young composers as 'competent agents in their own lives' (Holloway and Valentine, 2003: 16) by asking them to speak candidly to me about their compositional processes, the meanings they attach to this creative activity, and their feelings about confidence and skill levels in relation to composition and technology. I have adopted Alldred's (1998: 15) approach to working with young people, which offers 'a way of constructing children as active subjects, not objects, and of recognizing that they may have distinct perspectives on the world' (Alldred, 1998: 150). In interpreting the data, while aiming at all times to provide as balanced an account as possible, I recognize that 'there are no objective observations, only observations socially situated in the worlds of the observer and the observed' (Denzin and Lincoln, 1998: 24). Therefore, while my observation notes record the actualities of the situation as far as possible, the thoughts and interpretations that came out of these observations form part of my analysis as they impose certain principles of selection and organization.

Organization of the book

The book is organized into eight chapters. Chapter 2 is concerned with technological theories as they relate to the fields of gender and music technology, while Chapters 3 to 7 report the empirical findings. In Chapter 8 I offer some concluding remarks. A discussion of the relevant literature is integrated into the body of this book, whereby I put forward an argument for an interdisciplinary approach which draws together perspectives from the fields of sociology of technology, music education and feminist musicology.

In Chapter 2, drawing on perspectives from STS, I critically examine how technological determinist thinking underpins current policy on educational technology. I then highlight the ways in which the tenets of determinism can be discerned in current discussions about technology in the music classroom, suggesting that, despite claims for technology's democratizing potential, music technologies are not inclusive and the gendered discourses in operation in the music classroom go largely unobserved. I argue that taking a social constructivist approach to technology helps us to uncover the gendered dimensions of music technologies. Finally, drawing on feminist STS perspectives I critically look at the influence of Haraway's (1990/1985) 'cyborg' metaphor in understanding the relationship between women and technology and what it might mean to be a 'musical cyborg'.

Beginning my analysis of the empirical data, Chapter 3 explores the processes and practices that contribute to the gendered culture of the music technology classroom. It provides the context for understanding how institutional factors shape and are shaped by gender–technology relations. It aims to explore the nature of 'technological talk' and considers its impact in constructing gendered perceptions about boys' and girls' ways of learning about technology and technological confidence. I then offer a discussion of the processes that contribute to normative masculine expectations regarding how males control technology and technological information.

Chapter 4 examines in detail how the concept of technological expertise is constructed. I explore how the technological 'expert' is constructed and examine who is able to define what is and what counts as technological knowledge. I illustrate my arguments about the digital music classroom by highlighting the similarities found between the gendered social relations within the home and the workplace in order to show why males and females are positioned differently in relation to different technologies. This offers a much richer and more complex understanding of the gendering of technology, and provides the context in which to place my subsequent analysis. I argue that the dominant discourse of technological expertise and competence constructs a hegemonic technological masculinity which girls (and some boys) are unable and unwilling to adopt. I end this chapter with a discussion of how the gendering of music software is implicated in this process as it becomes positioned as a 'masculine' or 'feminine' technology.

Chapters 5 and 6 specifically focus on the composition process. Chapter 5 provides a discussion of the musical idea and the extent to which pupils are able to exercise autonomy in thinking up and developing their musical ideas. I examine how the gendered nature of teachers' involvement or 'interference' related to gendered perceptions of 'conformity' and 'nonconformity' in this part of the process can have a devastating effect on pupils' sense of ownership of their compositions. Chapter 6 looks at the extent to which pupils make use of technology for composition. I suggest that the computer itself can become a barrier to composition, with its focus on technological rather than musical mastery, and this has important implications for pupils' compositional identities.

Chapter 7 looks at some of the problems pupils face in negotiating technological spaces when composing. I suggest that, although historically and culturally women's compositional spaces have been confined to the private, domestic sphere, the reclamation of the private domain of the home may actually offer significant possibilities for young female composers to exercise greater agency in their approaches to writing music.

Finally, Chapter 8 summarizes the key themes and makes some suggestions for classroom practice.

Chapter 2
Challenging Technological Determinism in the Music Education Classroom

The impetus behind this book is a concern with the sociocultural contexts in which technologies are used, a perspective which is largely missing from current discussions about music education and technology. This results in a technocratic discourse that mirrors many of the tenets of technological determinism, a powerful orthodoxy that focuses on technology's so-called 'impact' on social change and social structures.

This chapter therefore has two main aims. Firstly, I offer a brief examination of the technological imperatives driving Britain's educational policy agenda, highlighting how the discourses in operation reflect a disturbing technological determinism that uncritically embraces technology's supposed transformative possibilities. These discourses reflect the widely held belief in the 'natural' and self-evident character of young people's engagement with technology in which youth and technology are routinely and unproblematically linked in policy discourses. I then go on to examine the reproduction of these discourses in the music technology classroom and put forward an argument for a more socially embedded understanding of music technology. As I observed in Chapter 1, research has shown significant differences in boys' and girls' types of technological engagement and levels of use underlining the importance of why we must be careful not to separate the technological from the social. Technology is always constituted in social practices, and these practices can be highly gendered. This is a central concern for those seeking to understand the relationship between gender and technology, particularly as the 'dissonance between promises of emancipation and the reality of the ways in which new technologies are distributed and controlled' (Henwood, Wyatt, Miller and Senker, 2000: 4) continue to present challenges for women in the fields of science and technology. Unless we counteract this unbridled determinism and engage with the social dimensions of the music classroom, it is likely that important and often troubling issues relating to gender will go unchallenged. While women have made some inroads into traditionally male dominated areas of music, musical cultures which have a strong technological focus such as music production, DJing and sound engineering have proved harder for women to break into (Sandstrom, 2000; Katz, 2004; Smaill, 2005) and they are still significantly underrepresented as composers in international events.[1] This draws our attention to why the gendered dimensions of music technology should be an important focus of study.

Stepulevage (2001) asserts that it is necessary not only to examine the process and practices that materially constitute gender–technology relations but to look at ways in which these relations can be reconfigured and challenged. Therefore, the aim of the final part of this chapter is to examine claims made for the technocultural construction of the 'musical cyborg', which some feminist musicologists suggest is a way of reconfiguring women's technological and bodily interactions in women's musical encounters. It has been argued that, when theorizing their relationship with machines, there is a tendency to veer between a 'pessimistic fatalism', whereby technological is viewed as oppressive to women, or 'utopian optimism', which views technology as inherently liberating (Wajcman, 2004: 103). This leads Wajcman (2004) to counsel for an approach which can bring together insights from cybercultural theory and the constructivist perspectives of STS, which the construction of the 'musical cyborg' claims to be able to do, and I will discuss both the strengths and limitations of appropriating this concept for women's engagement with music technologies.

Technological determinism and education policy

The pace of technological development has resulted in significant changes in how people work, and the nature of the work they undertake. Therefore, ensuring that people have the right kinds of skills has been identified as key to Britain's long-term economic prosperity and its ability to sustain a competitive advantage in the global economy (Leitch, 2006). This focus on technological change was an important driver for teaching and learning initiatives under the New Labour Government (1997–2010), which put ICT firmly at the centre of its educational policy. As a recent Ofsted report noted,

> Although, as yet, ICT is by no means at the heart of our education system, it is now widely recognized as an essential tool for learning in the twenty first century. Indeed, it is vital that today's children are enabled to take advantage of lifelong learning if they are to survive the constant pattern of change that is likely to mark their working lives. (Ofsted, 2004: 6)

In the era of the 'information age' the ability to adapt to the changes brought about by the 'ICT revolution' will enable us to 'cope with the demands of the digital economy and the complex and multiple "lifeworlds" of the next century' (Facer et al., 2001: 106). As Selwyn (2002) observes, to be 'unwired' is to be potentially

---

[1]   The 2010 programme for the BBC Proms concerts given at the Royal Albert Hall shows that, of the 144 composers performed during their summer concert series, only 6 were women.

disenfranchised, a position which feeds the concerns of parents who reason that investing in a home computer will ensure that their child, envisaged as a 'future worker', is not left behind (Holloway and Valentine, 2003), and which is echoed in young people's discourses in which the acquisition of computer skills is associated with successful careers and job opportunities (Ferrero, 2007). Consequently, the drive for greater digitization of the classroom since the mid-1990s is based on the premise that schools must ensure young people are adequately equipped with the necessary technological skills to enable them to respond to the pace of technological change that will characterize and impact on their working lives.

Underpinning such rhetoric is a belief that all pupils and teachers will want to engage with ICT, and it brooks no dissent that ICT-facilitated learning will lead to 'whole school improvement':

> The ICT in schools Divisional mission is to help all children achieve their full potential by supporting every school to become a centre of excellence in the use of ICT for teaching and learning and for whole school improvement. (DfES, 2003)

Unfortunately, when teachers argue that good teaching does not rely solely on the use of technology, this is perceived as an 'idiosyncratic rejection of technology' (Underwood et al., 2010: 19); teachers who voice concerns about this technocratic rhetoric, remaining unconvinced of the claims made for technology's educational potential, may find themselves derisorily referred to as a 'vociferous anti-technology lobby' (Underwood et al., 2010: 10). And yet, as Selwyn (2011: 22) notes, teachers are wise to be somewhat circumspect, because the 'compromised realities' of what actually happens in schools currently do not match the claims made for its potential, due to structural and material issues such as existing school infrastructure, pedagogy, and differing levels of professional ICT expertise amongst teaching staff.

What begins to emerge in current discourse is a conceptualization of educational ICTs as having the innate ability to transform both the social and educational experiences of young people, a discourse which uncritically reproduces a technological determinism which posits technology as an independent process, whereby technological change *determines* social and educational change.[2] In this formulation, not only is technology said to work independently from social forces but it is presented as a process of natural evolution, implying a predictability about its development and its 'effects'. Technologies are therefore assumed to have a natural trajectory, and their development and use cannot be challenged

---

[2]   Despite the technologically immersed 'cyberkid' of popular imagination, a recent BECTA (2008) survey found that 27 per cent of primary pupils and 17 per cent of secondary pupils did not have a computer at home. To this end the *Computers for Pupils* initiative launched by the Government in 2006 has so far invested £90 million in order to provide computers and internet access to children from disadvantaged homes with the dual aim of reducing the 'digital divide' and raising educational achievement.

or struggled over. Technological advances will happen automatically, thereby producing what May (2003) critically calls 'the myth of inevitability'. The orthodoxy of technological determinism, however flawed it might be, remains immensely powerful in contemporary society, and the phenomenal development and widespread availability of information, communication and digital technologies continue to fuel this 'myth'. A technologically determined orthodoxy can be detected in the early theorizing about the mass media as a natural sensory extension to ourselves, encapsulated in McLuhan's famous phrase 'the medium is the message', in which the 'message' of the medium or technology supposedly accelerates and changes human lives. Here the medium 'shapes and controls the scale and form of human association and actions' (1964: 9) and so the form in which the message is transmitted to us is supposedly more important than what is communicated. A similarly determinist position is repeated in Negroponte's (1995) assertion that, given what he sees as the 'transformative' powers of the Internet in the new 'information age', there is no alternative to being digital (Negroponte, 1995). May (2003: 4) sums up this lauding of digital technology as a belief that the 'information age becomes the explicit expression of inevitability, of progress, of the technological future made present'. May is right to be concerned: there is little room for social context within these determinist accounts, so to adopt such a position is to deny the possibility of self-determination; our existence is understood as little more than a series of events over which we apparently have no control. Unsurprisingly, this has been met by much concern, which May succinctly encapsulates when he expresses his fear that the current information society

> has become a wave which we can surf but cannot change or modify. This shift from engagement to passive accommodation has been accomplished by presenting these developments as epochal rather than taking place *within* contemporary society. (May, 2003: 3, italics in original)

What he sensibly highlights is that a refusal to acknowledge the social aspects of technology has serious consequences for society because it attributes a rationality to technology. Technology is consequently presented as the sole driving force for social change, a view that disregards any possibility for human agency and the active choices people make about their technological engagements.

This determinist trend in policy initiatives around educational technologies has recently come under scrutiny because of the way such policy reproduces what Stensaker et al. (2007) suggest is a 'normative perspective' which presupposes that ICT-based or ICT-supported learning will both improve and transform 'traditional' forms of teaching and learning. The newly emerging trend to incorporate Web 2.0 technologies into the classroom – where wikis, blogs, podcasts and social networking are being harnessed to enhance teaching and learning[3] – is a further

---

[3]   For recent discussion on the uses of Web 2.0 technologies in education see BECTA's (2009) report on e-books and the use of touch screens, Wang, Wu and Wang (2009) and the

example of this 'normative perspective'. There is an assumption that young people are using Web 2.0 technologies on a regular basis as part of their everyday social uses of the internet, and so incorporating them into the classroom is perceived almost as a natural progression from the informal to the formal setting. However, research suggests that, as yet, their use in formal educational settings is carried out in quite simple and unsophisticated ways requiring little more than basic technical skills in the majority of cases (Luckin et al., 2009) and yet, despite such findings, the level of technological investment has been considerable.[4] Moreover, this unquestioning acceptance of the revolutionary and transformative potential of ICTs has resulted in a worrying 'evangelizing' by policy-makers (Loader, 1998) whereby technology is offered as the 'solution' to a range of educational problems (Sefton-Green, 1998) ranging from improving poor behaviour and attendance to alleviating apparent disaffection with traditional forms of learning (Passey et al., 2003). Part of the thrust for greater investment in technology is underpinned by the government's focus on increasing pupil performance, attainment and motivation and yet, as numerous studies have shown, it is difficult to isolate ICT as the most significant variable when assessing educational outcomes (Pittard et al., 2003; Moss et al., 2006; Chandra and Lloyd, 2008) despite some more optimistic claims to the contrary (Passey et al., 2003). However, as a recent BECTA (2007) report acknowledges, such claims for the transformational possibilities of technology have not yet been achieved. While the Impact2 project (2002) found a positive relationship between ICT and pupil attainment at GCSE it makes the important point that, where there is quantifiable evidence, these improvements are not as a result of the technology per se but the ways in which teachers evaluate its fitness for purpose and make *effective* use of it in a given context. This is supported by the findings of the BECTA (2007) 'ICT Test Bed Evaluation', which noted that only when technology was properly embedded did national test outcomes rise.

Although the impact of technology on educational outcomes is inconclusive, the focus on technology-enhanced learning in the classroom remains central to all aspects of the curriculum, driven by the persistent representation within educational policy of children as habitually equated with 'the future' (Facer et al., 2001), a future that is presented as inexorably bound up in the technological and where ICT skills are viewed as essential for learning and life (Savage, 2007). To successfully progress into the workplace of the twenty-first century, characterized by an ever greater reliance on digital technologies, ICT is now deemed one of three 'functional skills', alongside English and mathematics, that pupils must acquire during their secondary school education (QCDA, 2010). However, it should be

---

use of mobile phones and the SMS messaging system, and Hew's (2009) helpful literature review of mobile technologies and the use of podcasts in educational settings.

[4]   In the UK, the primary sector alone now spends annually around £400 million on hardware, software and infrastructure (Cranmer, Potter and Selwyn, 2007). For the secondary sector this figure has been put at £332 million for hardware, infrastructure and associated software (Selwyn, 2011).

pointed out that technological hyberbole, or 'cyberbole' as Woolgar (2002) dubs it, is not entirely new, as the increased use of computers in the classroom has been on the political agenda since the 1980s, exemplified by the statement made in 1983 by the British MP Kenneth Baker:

> [*Children*] are my most devoted fellow missionaries. They are keen, willing, and rapidly becoming expert. It is a children's crusade that is leading us into the Information Technology Revolution. (cited in Haddon and Skinner, 1991: 438)

What is noticeable is that the rhetoric since that time consistently reinforces the notion of the 'natural' connection between children and technologies which, in more recent accounts, presents an unproblematic portrayal of children as 'digital natives' (Prensky, 2001). Those born since 1980, dubbed the 'net generation' (Tapscott, 1998), are a generation whose lives are said to be intrinsically bound up and transformed by digital technologies.[5] More recently, Prensky has replaced his idea of the 'digital native' with that of the 'digital human' (Prensky, 2009). In this depiction, the 'digital human' will come to accept that, in order to overcome the apparent limitations of their digitally unenhanced mind due to the limited processing powers of the human brain, the 'digital human' will come to understand that digital 'enhancement' will be an integral part of human existence. In this envisaged future, the potential afforded by the 'enhanced mind' is only achievable through engagement with digital technologies. This veneration of the technological is deeply troubling because it focuses solely on what are believed to be technology's innately transformative possibilities. It is important that these taken-for-granted assumptions are challenged because they fail to take into account the active choices that young people make about the media with which they engage (Livingstone, 2002). Uncritically celebrating the claims made for digital technology as 'liberating', 'empowering' and 'democratizing', offering unparalleled possibilities for children's creativity merely perpetuates myths about the so-called 'digital generation' because it does not acknowledge disparities regarding use and accessibility of technologies or the different social, economic and political contexts of their use (Buckingham and Willetts, 2006). These discourses are underpinned by the notion that ICT is inherently motivating and, as Selwyn (2008: 18) observes, 'commentators are often driven by assumptions of the allure of new media for young people rather than empirical evidence', reinforcing what Freedman (2003: 185) believes is an erroneous 'common sense' view of digital systems as innately democratizing.

---

[5]   See Buckingham (2007) for a critical discussion of both Tapscott and Prensky.

Challenging determinist discourses in the technologized music classroom

The appropriation of music technologies by musicians and composers working in both popular and Western Classical traditions has a long and varied history (Taylor, 2001), but the use of digital technologies in electronic dance culture[6] and young people's informal musical practices is more recent (Whiteley et al., 2004). The appropriation of digital technologies into the music classroom aims to reflect these informal practices, as outlined in the National Curriculum for Music, which cites a range of digital technologies for use in music composition. These are said to help pupils capture, manipulate and combine sounds in order to create melodies and harmonies, and to develop rhythmic ideas within a range of musical styles. While music technologies may offer interesting pedagogic possibilities, the social dimensions of their use are rarely addressed. There is a worrying tendency to focus too narrowly on the motivational and democratizing qualities of music technology, taking a 'technology as hardware' view in which technology is presented as devoid of social context. This asocial characterization mainly focuses on technology's inherent ability to effect change but ignores the cultural context in which it is used, which includes the teacher's role, their level of expertise, existing pedagogic practices (Burnard, 2007), and pupils' attitudes towards technology. Drawing on data collated from recent Ofsted inspections of secondary school music lessons into what characterizes good teaching with ICT, Mills and Murray (2000) make the salient point that, while ICT during Key Stage 3[7] is a curriculum requirement, there are aspects of the National Curriculum that can be effectively taught without ICT. Although music ICT can support learning and increase motivation in some cases, in 'good' music teaching 'ICT was not allowed to take over the role of the teacher' (Mills and Murray, 2000: 134). Despite this cautionary note, some of their subsequent comments unintentionally replicate the rhetoric of determinism asserting that ICT offers all young composers wider creative possibilities because pupils are no longer limited by their inability to notate or play their compositions. This perspective is reiterated by Hodges (1996), who stated that new technologies can 'liberate' composers. Because the software can give immediate aural feedback, the composer is no longer dependent on their own music skills.

This perspective appears to be increasingly common currency in the music education literature that posits music technology as having an inevitable and usually beneficial impact on how pupils compose. The literature uncritically lauds

---

[6]   For interesting cultural accounts of electronic dance cultures see St John (2001) for a discussion of the Australian scene, and Gilbert and Pearson (1999) for a wide-ranging discussion around identity and meaning in the technologized dance scene. Technology has also changed the ways in which we produce, distribute and consume music, and Théberge (1997) provides an interesting, if somewhat overly determinist, perspective.

[7]   Key Stages are the main areas into which the National Curriculum for schools is divided: Key Stage 1 (5–7-year-olds); Key Stage 2 (7–11-year-olds); Key Stage 3 (11–14-year-olds) and Key Stage 4 (14–16-year-olds).

technology's 'transformative' aspects and its 'democratizing' and 'empowering' potential (Hodges, 1996; Phillips and Pearson, 1997; Rogers, 1997; Folkestad et al., 1998; Hodges, 2001) asserting that pupils achieve greater compositional 'success' when using music technology (Savage and Challis, 2001; 2002). Reporting on a large-scale curriculum-based music project in which Key Stage 3 pupils were asked to compose an electroacoustic piece using a range of technologies, Savage and Challis (2001) were interested in implementing 'innovative' uses of ICT that would enhance teaching and learning in music. Their stated aim for the project was 'to attempt to demonstrate the empowering and facilitating nature these new technologies can have for all pupils when used imaginatively and constructively in the classroom' (Savage and Challis, 2001: 140). Many pupils within the project clearly did find some of the technologies useful, especially those that provided a wider range of sounds than was normally available and those that enabled new ways of manipulating sounds such as the software ProTools, a digital audio mixing programme that works in a similar way to that of a traditional multi-track tape recorder. However, although a wide range of software and hardware was made available to the pupils, it became apparent that some were too difficult to master given the project's time frame. This led Savage and Challis to conclude that the impetus behind the use of these technologies was related to their accessibility and ease of use irrespective of the creative possibilities they may have offered. They ultimately deemed the project a 'success' because they claimed the different technologies used 'empowered the majority of pupils' (2001: 147). However, no mention is made of the implied 'minority' who were presumably not 'empowered'. Their notion of 'empowerment' is somewhat obscure and rather narrowly defined. They claim that the technologies had a positive impact because pupil empowerment was judged by the degree to which pupils 'did not rely on a traditional grounding in instrumental skills' (2001: 146) and the extent to which pupils were able to develop more sophisticated musical thinking given this set of technological tools. Their argument produces a technocratic discourse that not only ignores differences in pupils' approaches and aptitude in this type of compositional setting but also appears to place higher value on digitally mediated processes because of what it enables pupils to do in contrast to more 'traditional' methods. Similarly, Hickey (1997) observes that the traditional music classroom may not be the most conducive environment for creative work. She suggests that computer-mediated composition, where pupils can work independently without constant monitoring by the teacher and not having to perform their work to others, provides a non-evaluative, safe environment for pupils who appear unmotivated and are not regarded as competent composers in a more traditional setting.[8] In

---

[8] Classroom composition has often been carried out as a group activity, and Pitts and Kwami (2002) express their disquiet that music software packages may diminish group music-making in the virtual reality of the computer room. In contrast, Odam (2000) has been critical of the amount of group work used in composition lessons, highlighting the potential problems regarding individual assessment and ensuring the development of

their discussion of compositional strategies, Folkestad (1998) and Folkestad et al. (1998) employ a similar argument, suggesting that all pupils within their studies 'succeeded' in creating a piece of music, leading them to assert that composition is no longer the preserve of the gifted few (which, if this is the case, is of course welcomed). There is insufficient critical exploration, from the pupils' perspective, whether they really are as beneficial or as democratizing as they assert. However, they do offer a small caveat to these blanket claims noting that different types of software might affect ways of creating music. For example, the type of interface or inputting device (usually a keyboard) might be more helpful to some pupils than others might be, and may restrict musical ideas, steering the music into a different direction than previously intended.

Airy and Parr (2001) are a little more circumspect about the unquestioned benefits of music technology, arguing that the supposed advantages of MIDI technology reported in the literature are based on generalized and unsubstantiated claims about its efficacy and democratizing potential. Their own work places pupils' experiences at the centre of their investigation into MIDI use, recognizing that there is difference and diversity in pupils' use of the compositional technology. For example, within the MIDI sequencing environment four different interfaces, via different editors, are provided so that in each window the same data is displayed but in different formats, and pupils in their study made explicit choices about which editor they preferred to work with. Those with formal musical training found that the notation editor was most useful, while those with little music-reading ability found the matrix editor useful, because pupils can lengthen or shorten notes without worrying about writing down the actual note values. They also observe that the most commonly used MIDI controller (through which musical ideas are played into the computer) was the keyboard, but those lacking keyboard skills found it a major barrier to composition. Drummers, who use hands and feet, experience significant difficulties in having to externalize their ideas through this medium, suggesting that these considerations must be taken into account when expecting pupils to adopt a wholly computer-mediated approach to composition.

Acknowledging the social

What the above demonstrates is that the rhetoric of 'inevitability' strongly permeates discussions about music technologies: a compositional medium that is purported to have a positive impact on pupils' working processes, and by which compositional 'success' is assured for all pupils. As discussed earlier with

individual skills as pupils can 'hide' their lack of skills in group work. Glover (2000) makes a similar point, arguing that progress is faster and learning is more secure when children are given opportunities to compose on their own. This is also supported by Hickey's (1997) belief that individualized learning in a computer environment offers more 'authentic' creative music-making activities.

regard to educational ICT policy, the danger here is that this rhetoric reinforces technological determinist interpretations of children's use and relations to ICT, their positioning as 'natural' users obscuring difference and inequality (Holloway and Valentine, 2003). This serves to emphasize why it remains imperative to develop a sociological understanding of young people and their use of digital technologies in the music classroom. Within current educational policy there appears to be an uncritical assumption that 'all ICT is good ICT', in which the learner her/himself as a socially constituted subject warrants little or no attention. Unfortunately, this focus on 'impacts' pays insufficient attention to the educational context into which technology is incorporated or how it is used by teachers and pupils. As Moran-Ellis and Cooper (2000) rightly observe, this type of simplistic formulation underpins much of the current UK Government policy regarding ICT and educational policies, with its focus on computer literacy and access. As they go on to say, 'the fundamental flaw in such claims derives from the decontexualising … of ICT from cultural and social relationships' (2000: 4). This underlines why Winner (1977) is right to assert that the concept of determinism is far too sweeping in its implications to provide an adequate theory for understanding technology's relationship to society. It does little justice to the genuine choices that arise, in both principle and practice, in the course of technical and social transformation. Paying attention to the social dimensions of technology results in a shift away from the notion of technology as an autonomous driving force that will impact and shape society to an incorporation and acknowledgement of the social factors that shape technology.

While critical of technological determinist perspectives, Winner does not deny the importance of technological innovation but argues that the fundamental problem arises when one tries to isolate individual 'causes' attributed to social change. It is impossible to prove that any one factor, in this case technology, could be *the* primary determinant. He makes the interesting point that there have been periods in history where advances in scientific and technical knowledge did not have a profound effect on social practice because the social conditions were not appropriate. He cites the Alexandrian inventions of the second and third centuries BC in which primitive versions of both the steam engine and the wheeled cart appeared but neither was taken up because, at the time, these technologies had little use within the social and economic context of Alexandrian society. Winner points out that 'patterns of technology are themselves influenced by the conditions in which they exist' (1977: 76). He is therefore not arguing for a rejection of the importance of technological innovation but advocating a more dialectical approach to understanding technology: that it is both a determinant of and is determined by the society in which it exists. Technologies therefore *reflect* and *affect* the surrounding social conditions (Bromley and Apple, 1998). Acknowledging the social dimensions of technology incorporates the human choices that produce the dynamics and direction of technologies (Mumford, 1934; Williams, 1974; May, 2003). Technology's 'social embeddedness' is what counts; the interaction between human beings and technology means that there is no 'natural' one-dimensional trajectory, no foreclosed future that we cannot change: 'There is no such thing as *the* future; there are many, many futures. And our concern should be with what the future ought to be, what we want it to be' (Sardar, cited by May 2003: 6, italics in original). Rather than having to adapt to technological change, we can start to think about the role played by society in shaping technological development and use, thereby taking what can be seen as a broadly 'social constructivist' approach (Mackenzie and Wajcman, 1985).

An example of this is found in the early work of Pinch and Bijker (1989) and their Social Construction of Technology (SCOT) approach, whereby different meanings and interactions come to be associated with distinct social groups. Theirs was one of the first attempts to define the 'relevant social groups' involved in the development of a technological artefact and the meanings that different social groups associated with it, highlighting the interpretive flexibility of the artefact. In their research into the development of the 'Rudge Ordinary' bicycle, for example, Pinch and Bijker noted that the meanings attributed to the bicycle were differently configured depending on whether the user was male, female, young or old. Young men tended to view the bicycle as a daring, exciting 'macho machine' ideal for sporting purposes, whereas women and elderly riders interpreted the design as dangerous and unsafe, unsuitable for general transport. Moreover, its size and design made it difficult for women to ride given their generally smaller size and mode of dress. While a SCOT perspective offers a more nuanced understanding of technology, it is important to recognize that these groups do not exist within a social vacuum, and the decisions they make about technology reflect their own values and expectations, which may reproduce gendered discourses about technology.

An important aspect of examining the social dimension of technology has been its ability to show how dominant groups assert and maintain power over other groups in their technological interactions, and is a central concern for feminist research. Murray (1993) argues that men's conscious control of technology comes from a deeper motive to protect a masculine reality which has been secured in the symbolic significance of technology. Understanding the socially constructed aspect of technology–gender relations helps us to uncover the discourses that often make it difficult for women to influence or participate in the development and use of technologies. As Wajcman observes,

> Because social groups have different interests and resources, the development process brings out conflicts between different views of the technical requirements of the device. Accordingly, the stability and form of artefacts depends on the capacity and resources that the salient social groups can mobilize in the course of the development process … [*therefore*] what they overlook is the fact that the absence of influence from certain groups may also be significant … The almost complete exclusion of women from the technological community points to the need to take account of the underlying structures of gender relations. Preferences

for different technologies are shaped by a set of social arrangements that reflect
men's power in the wider society. (Wajcman, 1991: 23–4)

Her observation about women's exclusion from the technological community
also alerts us to another limitation of Pinch and Bijker's formulation of social
groups, because their empirical identification of those groups was carried
out by examining historical documents. Therefore, groups not mentioned in
these documents are deemed not to have any input into the development of the
technological artefact, which is highly significant because, while women have
historically made important contributions to the field of science and technology
(Watts, 2007; Beyer, 2009), their contributions have often gone unacknowledged.
Focusing solely on the groups represented in historical accounts of technological
developments, accounts in which women will be largely absent, is likely to
reinforce the perception of women as neither interested nor sufficiently skilled
to contribute to technological developments, rather than seeing their invisibility
as socially and historically produced. As feminist STS researchers such as Linn
(1987) rightly point out, labelling something as 'technology has more to do with
who is using it, in what statused context' (1987: 134); therefore, as I argued in
Chapter 1, viewing technology as a cultural practice rather than a 'thing' helps
uncover why there continue to be gendered differences in access to technology,
in the recognition of technical skills, and the acknowledgement of women's
contributions to technological developments.

Theorizing women's interactions with music technologies

Although women do enter areas of the music industry strongly associated with
technology, such as the record industry, they may find themselves in low-paid,
unskilled or semi-skilled jobs that carry very little status or power, as often the
most prestigious jobs are occupied by men (Bayton, 1998). Although Cunningham
notes that women DJs are becoming more common, far fewer go on to become
record producers, achieving this greater level of technological status. It has been
argued that this gendering of technological skill and men's appropriation of tools
and machinery are 'an important source of women's subordination, indeed it is
part of the process by which females are constituted as women' (Cockburn, 1999b:
181). This suggests that the material and symbolic distinctions between male and
female expertise remain intact, and institutional factors contribute to the continuing
identification of technology with masculinity that results in men still having more
opportunities than women in the world of composition and engineering (Goodwin,
cited in Cunningham, 1998: 148). Even when they are working in technological
spaces on an equal footing with their male counterparts, women encounter serious
challenges. Being only one of four women in a composition class of thirty, a
respondent in McCartney's (1995) study noted that the women who did remain on
the course did not identify themselves 'as women' and were often very isolated,

not even talking to other women very much because, as one participant observed, they had to 'prove themselves all the time they were there. So they didn't identify themselves as women, so I didn't have the feeling that they were there, [*even though*] they were' (1995: 11). When women found themselves in the minority, their experiences could often be very negative:

> I didn't know anything about computers when I started … I was in a class with eleven men, and they all seemed to be really hip to what was going on. There was a strong air of aggression in the class – probably all blustering, since I doubt that many of them knew much about computers either … Somehow I survived that environment and learnt by spending hours in the studio. (Composition student Wende Bartley in McCartney, 1995: 8–9)

Feeling they have to adapt and conform to male norms and expectations is also an issue for female pupils in the music technology classroom. Caputo (1994) argues that cultural assumptions about technology can result in valuing more 'malestream' forms of digital knowledge such as mastery of skills and rational, linear processes – forms of thought that produce a mechanistic way of thinking. Caputo argues that this means that girls either have to conform to these ways of thinking or remain silenced because girls' socialization encourages relational, analogic ways of knowing that do not fit working with information in a digital format in the 'malestream' way she describes. Consequently, 'girls are set up for failure on some level as they confront technology and are measured by a male norm' (1994: 89). 'Fitting in' therefore not only requires women to adopt an identity that does not call attention to their femininity but also requires adapting to 'masculine' ways of working in a digital culture that privileges male ways of knowing.

Whereas engaging with technology is affirmatory of masculinity, women's engagement with it marks an interruption to their femininity because technological expertise is not part of feminine identity. Consequently, as outlined in Chapter 1, Green (1997) argues that this is why women singers are acceptable in a way that women composers are not, because notions of the 'feminine' are reduced to the physical, 'natural' body in the former but not the latter. This stands in contrast to the body of the female instrumentalist which, although still on display, is now mediated through a piece of technology. Unlike the woman musician, the singing woman's body is the source of the sound and does not require any external intervention: 'The body is the instrument. The singing woman is, literally and metaphorically, in tune with her body' and the absence of technology 'affirms patriarchal definitions of femininity' (Green 1997: 28).[9] This is not the case with composition, which involves no corporeal mediation, but requires 'knowledge and control of compositional technique'. Composition is therefore symbolically linked to the mind, and becomes part of an affirmatory masculine identity, and identity not grounded in the corporeal.

Grosz (1994) maintains that the crisis in conceptions of knowledge and knowledge production has resulted from the historical privileging of the mental over the corporeal. The knower has been conceptualized as disembodied and this knower is male. She states that men have taken on the role of neutral knowers and thinkers because they have 'evacuated their own specific forms of corporeality and repressed all traces of their sexual specificity from the knowledges they produce' (1994: 204). She further argues that we cannot ignore this explicit sexualization of knowledges, asserting that there is a distinct relationship that models of knowledge have to sexually specific (male) bodies. She rejects the notion of the male body as the main site of knowledge production and attempts to reclaim the female body, arguing it is this specificity that provides a site of possible resistance. Grosz wants to develop the female body as the *subject* of knowledge that will reveal the phallocentric and partial nature of dominant knowledges as well as creating new ways of knowing. Rather than attempting to either omit the body or even transcend it, Grosz wants to put the body first, right at the centre of subjectivity. It is not enough for women to be involved in gaining access to knowledge but they must help in creating that knowledge, making their own meanings (Green et al., 1993). Adam (1998), in her discussion of the body in Artificial Intelligence, makes similar observations. She notes that in the artificial world of cyberspace, where the mind is downloaded into a robot, there is an assumption that the body can be left behind. She suggests that much of cyberspace's appeal for men is through these masculine attempts to transcend and escape 'the meat' (the body). By questioning the superiority of the archetypal knower, a universal male subject, and insisting that we look for meanings in terms of embodiment via real bodies in the real

---

⁹   Frith (1996: 192) makes the same observation by stating that 'the voice *is* the sound of the body'; the reason the voice is expressive of the body is precisely because it gives the listener access to it without mediation. Barthes (1977) uses the idea of the 'grain' of the voice to signify the relationship between a singer and the body, in which the 'grain' is the materiality of the body. Different timbral qualities have differential bodily implications and Frith (1996) suggests that the 'ungrained' voice would suggest a voice that conceals its own means of physical production. This ideology of the singing woman as associated with the body is reproduced in Adorno's (1928) essay on the phonograph in which he claims that a woman's singing voice could not be recorded as well as a man's voice. He asserts that the former demands the physical presence of her body while the absence of a body in the latter is not considered problematic in the same way. Without a body, the female voice is 'needy and incomplete'. The male voice, however, projects a self that is identical with its sound and therefore more amenable to phonographic reproduction.

world, feminists will be able to challenge the 'stereotypical mould', providing the possibility for a different type of knower.

Transcending the corporeal in women's technological interactions

The privileging of the 'masculine' mind over the 'feminine' body remains a continuing concern in recent feminist discussions of the gendering of technology, and yet these gendered associations are deeply ingrained in the social and cultural contexts of technological interactions. This tenacious link between masculinity and technology has necessitated the use of new tools to understand this relationship, and recent theorizing about women's engagement with technology has looked to Haraway's (1990) influential, yet controversial, notion of the 'cyborg', which is proffered as an alternative way of conceptualizing women's participation in the construction of new meanings in the world of technology. Haraway offers her postmodern metaphor of the cyborg, which brings together the human and the machine, as a feminist critique of technology and women within contemporary capitalist and patriarchal society which she believes is 'faithful to feminism, socialism, and materialism' (1990: 190). As such, this 'creature of social reality as well as a creature of fiction' (1990: 191) has become a widely used rhetorical device for some feminists commentators. With its utopian vision of a gender-free future, the cyborg appears to offer the potential for a reconstructed female identity that supposedly transcends the corporeal and challenges cultural assumptions about males and females. Its influence on feminist cybercultural theory requires some discussion.

While Davis (1997) believes cyborgs may offer new ways of thinking about women in the digital domain, she draws our attention to the fact that this can lead to an abstraction of the body from concrete social contexts that lead to a disjuncture between the symbolic and the material:

> While there has been a wealth of feminism scholarship devoted to exploring the particularities of embodiment, recent feminist theory on the body has displayed a marked ambivalence towards the material body and a tendency to privilege the body as metaphor. (Davis, 1997: 15)

The problem Davis has acknowledged is particularly pertinent given that cybercultural theory about female bodies, identity and technology seems less concerned with dismantling the *mechanisms* through which women are discouraged from engaging with technology than the *symbolic* meanings associated with female cyborgs. As Davis observes, by divorcing the symbolic from the material so sharply and not addressing the concrete social spaces between the two, it will be difficult to develop embodied theories of the body that are able to challenge patriarchal systems. It is this contradiction and tension between Haraway's cyborg as a disembodied, socially unencumbered construct and the corporeal embodied subject in the production of knowledge that seems to be the stumbling block to political engagement, despite her vision of the cyborg as having the potential for political mobilization.

Cultural representations of cyborgian identities often retain the 'essences' of the dual nature of the human–machine hybrid. Although the cyborg is predominantly understood as a machine (it is programmed, does not show emotion), in visual representations it must retain elements of its 'human-ness' and with it other physically and culturally inscribed markers of sex and gender which cyberbodies in popular culture often exaggerate (Springer, 1999). These cultural associations cannot be eclipsed or effaced but end up merely reproducing extreme constructions of masculinity and femininity. For example, the ultimate cyborg as exemplified in the film *The Terminator* (James Cameron, 1984) is presented as a male body, barely human but very obviously male with its sculpted muscles and imposing physical size. Springer notes that, even though the male body has been replaced with electronic parts and as such has been deconstructed, this reconfigured technological masculinity does not disrupt existing gendered hierarchies:

> In a world without human bodies … technological things will be gendered and there will still be a patriarchal hierarchy. What this reconfiguration of masculinity indicates is that patriarchy is more willing to dispense with human life than with male superiority. (Springer, 1999: 48–9)

Female gendered cyborgs also inhabit traditional feminine roles and are endowed with stereotypically feminine traits. The female cyborg 'Rachel' in the film *Bladerunner* (Ridley Scott, 1982) inhabits a sexually inscribed body that is the object of the male human Deckard's desire, which 'symbolically reasserts the social and political position of woman as object of man's consumption' (Balsamo, 1999: 148). Despite this stereotyped image, Balsamo maintains that female cyborg images are more able to challenge the opposition between humans and machines because 'femininity is less compatible with technology than is masculinity … because our cultural imagination aligns masculinity and rationality with technology and science, male gendered cyborgs fail to radically challenge the distinction between human and machine' (1999: 149).

Balsamo (1999) asserts that the cultural contradictions embodied in the *female* cyborg strain the technological imagination precisely because the cyborg typically represented in popular culture is aligned with masculinity and male expertise. This leads her to suggest that these contradictions transform the masculine connotations normally associated with cyborgs, which in turn offer the possibility of reconfiguring existing gender–technology relations. I would suggest that these cultural contradictions are less easy to read than she believes; the dominant reading when we look at the female cyborg is her 'essential' femininity, sexuality and objectification. More often than not, this is the most noticeable thing about her. Similarly, the image of 'Lara Croft', a computer-generated heroine in the popular *Tomb Raider* game, might be interpreted as an attempt to present an empowered female identity (physically strong, aggressive, fearless). However, her bodily image, with its small waist, long slim legs and large breasts, merely grounds Lara in an idealized feminine identity that instantly marks her out as female carrying with it all the cultural baggage that goes with such an eroticized and sexualized representation. The game even features a 'Nude Raider' patch that removes Lara's clothing, making it rather difficult to conceive of Lara as the feminist heroine some claim her to be (Wajcman, 2004). Despite attempts to use the concept of the cyborg as a way of rethinking women's relationship with the technological, the cyborg body is no more likely to be free of social constraints than the corporeal body. Traditional gendered roles are rarely challenged in visual representations of cyborgs, so the cyborg is as much of a construct as the corporeal 'woman' and one must therefore ask if a reconstructed body can really guarantee a reconstructed cultural identity (Gonzalez, 2000). Balsamo (1999) asserts that the cyborg image merely reproduces limiting not liberating stereotypes of gender and sexuality. So, in light of these reservations, in what ways can a cyborgian subjectivity be potentially transformative? Balsamo's (1999) reading of the cyborg is helpful in this regard, in her conception of it as a symbol for interpreting how old and new technologies and old and new identities can work together. She envisages the assemblage of the female as parts of women's experiences that can be reassembled in such a way that seeks to ground the female cyborg in a material sense. Unfortunately, a purely symbolic representation does little to disrupt the material constraints faced by women in their technological encounters.

Musical cyborgs

Although the above alerts us to the limitations of the cyborg for reconfiguring gender social relations, it is of interest that the construction of a 'musical cyborg' has been put forward as providing a way of examining women's engagement with technology in musical spaces in ways that can be deemed empowering. One such example is Dickinson's (2001) discussion of the use of a vocoder on Cher's hit single *Believe* (1998).[10] The vocoder came to prominence in the 1970s when synthesized music was very popular but has had resurgence as the 'Cher effect' (as this vocoded sound was dubbed) can be detected in the songs of a number of female artists including Madonna, Christina Aguilera, Faith Hill and Kylie Minogue. Dickinson (2001) argues that the recent appropriation of the vocoder

---

[10]   There are two kinds of vocoder. The first modifies the pitch and is useful for pitch corrections; the second uses the input signal to modify a given carrier signal, producing a robotic-sounding voice. There is now some controversy over whether or not a vocoder was used on this track, as it is now widely believed that the producers in fact used 'auto tune' software to create this effect. For an account of the recording process, see *Sound on Sound* (1999) www.soundonsound.com/sos/feb99/articles/tracks661.htm (accessed 23 October 2010).

by female popular music artists may create potentially empowering new meanings for this piece of music technology, helping us to rethink the role of recording technologies in the construction of female musical corporeality. Drawing on Green's (1997) assertion that, for female singers, the body is their instrument, Dickinson observes that the involvement of the body is ever present in popular music and discourse, but the 'naturalism' of the female singing voice is impaired and confuses the listener as to its origin when heard through a vocoder. Therefore the vocoder is now more readily conjoined with the feminized voice and thus offers the 'cyber potential' of an empowered digitalized female identity.

However, her claims appear to be a powerful example of the problems of privileging the symbolic over the material as noted earlier by Balsamo (1999), who stresses that a cyborgian subjectivity can only achieve material transformation when grounded in women's actual experiences. Dickinson quotes from an interview by Mark Taylor (one of the producers of the track) at length about the recording process but omits a crucial aspect of his narrative (from the same interview) in which Taylor is reported as saying 'It was a bit radical … Basically, it was the total destruction of her voice, so I was really nervous about playing it to her.'[11] Cher's disembodied voice now becomes the raw material for Taylor's technological manipulations. Dickinson (2001) is very much aware that her argument might be challenged on these grounds, at one point asking if the knowledge that the record was produced by two men undermines the power she ascribes to 'vocoded female articulacy' (2001: 342). Somewhat unsatisfactorily she sidesteps this issue by asserting that, as female vocalists often feature within dance music in supporting roles (Bradby, 1993), the fact that the female Cher is established at the helm is sufficient warrant for her to make her assertion. Indeed, Cher's status as a successful female pop singer is likely to ensure that this was the case. So, what does this have to do with technology? When we see Cher performing, in all her sexualized, cosmetically modified glory, is she really the 'metaphor for what women could possibly achieve with more prestigious forms of technology' (Dickinson, 2001: 341) given that we know she had little input in the technological processes that went into the modification of her voice? Within this context, can we accept Dickinson's claim of the vocoder as a 'symbolic bridge' between perceptions of humans and machines? Perhaps it is possible to make this assertion if we draw on Balsamo's (1999) observation that female gendered cyborgs (in this case, Cher) are better able to challenge existing technological discourses because we do not normally associate femininity and women with technology. However, I think this is still rather tenuous. Dickinson (2001) acknowledges that music technologies are also systems of control, but she appears reluctant to engage with this aspect of material subjectivity. Dickinson does begin to acknowledge this dilemma when she describes the process that Mark Taylor went through to achieve the desired effect, but she still sees fit to assert that the incorporation of the vocoder in women's vocal performances

---

[11]   Full interview found at www.soundonsound.com/sos/feb99/articles/tracks66.htm.

attributes mastery to a woman, even if she was not part of that particular production process ... Even if the vocal manoeuvre was not negotiated by 'the real Cher', she does become a metaphor for what women could possibly achieve with more prestigious forms of technology ... A vocoder intervenes at an unavoidable level of *musical* expression ... encouraging the listener to think of these women as professionals within music practice. (Dickinson, 2001: 341)

I would argue that, rather than being an active part and a challenge to these existing practices, the material, embodied Cher appears to have been subsumed within a system of musical production which is man-made and male-controlled; a situation which women in popular music continue to find themselves. It is important to be clear about the level of intentionality before making claims for Cher's 'empowerment': 'the person engaging in resistant acts must do so consciously and be able to relate that consciousness and intent' (LeBlanc, cited by Piano, 2003). Having identified Cher's exclusion from the mode of production, Dickinson (2001) chooses to ignore this by focusing on what Cher *represents* as opposed to her actual technological manipulation of her own voice. Creating a 'false' separation between the technological representations of Cher's voice from the actual practice of its technological manipulation by two male producers does not make a convincing argument for Cher's supposed technological empowerment. In reality, the incorporation of a piece of voice manipulating technology does not reflect what Cher might actually 'mean' to the observer, which one presumes will inevitably focus on her embodied presence.

A similar issue arises in Loza's (2001) discussion of 'digital sound divas' in the world of electronic dance music, in which she makes a distinction between the fluid cyborg conjured up by Haraway which she believes *can* take up an ardent feminist position, and the conventionally sexed cyborg or 'fembot'. This fembot is the feminized machine that rearticulates and encapsulates sexual stereotypes and is firmly under male control. Loza describes the 'sensual sighs and simulated cries' of Donna Summer in the 'disco orgasm' *Love to Love you Baby* in which the male music producer, Giorgio Moroder, is able to control artificially Donna Summer's 'fembot', eliciting what Loza calls a 'pornosonic confession that concomitantly testified to his mastery of nascent computer technologies and female sexuality' (2001: 351). The musical fembot continues to represent sonically a sexualized version of the female which, rather than interrogating multiple dualities (as might the political cyborg of Haraway's imagination) actually resurrects binary borders.

In contrast, Grosz (1993) argues that we must aim to reconceptualize the body for feminists in such a way that it cannot be charged with essentialism and the reproduction of sexual stereotypes. She sees the body as an inscriptive surface on which social law, morality and values are inscribed. She states that bodies speak because they become coded as signs; as such, they speak social codes. Therefore, like the 'real' body, the 'cyber' body bears upon it the marks of its culture. What it looks like, its shape, its gendered characteristics contribute to a semiotic body which can be 'read' and to which social and gendered meanings are ascribed. This is illustrated by Bradby's (1993) description of the sampling of one woman's voice and another's body within the 1989 song *Ride on Time* produced by the Italian group Black Box. The vocals had been sampled from a song by an American soul singer, Loleatta Holloway (an older, maternal-looking woman), but the video that accompanied the song showed Katherine Quinol, a younger, sexier woman 'performing' the vocals rendering Holloway's unacceptable maternal body invisible. This invisibility was reinforced by the fact that Holloway's 'contribution' (her voice) was not originally credited. Here, the technology itself is seen as producing this dichotomy, as sampling involves considerable changes to the original sound so it becomes difficult to ascertain where the original recording ends and the sampled version begins. Holloway was accused of not understanding the new technology as if this were sufficient reason for not crediting her contribution. But, as Green (1997) observes, it is doubtful if Quinol herself 'understood technology' either, but she was not expected to as the focus was on the display of her body, the sexually, desirable body and object of the male gaze as opposed to Holloway's undesirable, maternal body. While acknowledging that the separation of one woman's voice credited separately from the visual image of another female body is unacceptable, Bradby (1993: 171) does suggests that the resultant cyborg of this technologization may have some positive implications for women in pop music. The cyborgian female image, via Quinol's body, appears to reinforce Balsamo's (1999) concerns that the female cyberbody retains its cultural markers of gender and sexuality. However, Bradby (1993: 171) suggests that, at the level of representation, this juxtaposition of the body and voice of two women may challenge what she calls 'the primacy of the visual in our everyday imaging of the body (which has been central to feminist analysis of the representation of women)'. Because the singing appears 'disembodied' and is no longer rooted in a body we can see, the singing voice's location in plural bodies offers a cyborgian representation of the female body that can be seen and heard differently, perhaps turning out to be a technological amalgam that does offer the possibility for rethinking gendered identities.

While these theoretical perspectives offer interesting interpretations of women's encounters with music technology, too little attention is paid to their material input, the focus resting largely on what these supposed 'musical cyborgs' represent. If we are to make claims for technology's empowerment of women, we have to acknowledge the extent to which they are free to exercise control over their bodies, voices and music-making. The performance artist Laurie Anderson is perhaps the most convincing of all 'musical cyborgs' because she is fully in control of manipulating and defining what counts as technology and music, developing new technologies and gadgets for her performances. As McClary (1991) observes, in Anderson's work the female body is at the centre of her electronically saturated performance space. The relationship with technological is not merely metaphorical but materially embodied. As Anderson herself states:

All of my work that deals with machines, and how they talk and think, is inherently critical. That's certainly the bias. But I think many people have missed an important fact: those songs themselves are made up of digital bits. My work is expressed through technology – a lot of it depends on 15 million watts of power. (Laurie Anderson, cited in McClary, 1991: 137)

All of Anderson's work focuses around new media and technology, from electronic opera to inventing musical instruments, merging theatre and technology, 'a theatre where technology becomes an organic extension of voice, body and space' (Jestrovic, 2002), where the borderline between the body and machine is blurred. In the performance of *Home of the Brave* Anderson dons a suit with built-in electronic sensors that are activated as she moves so that her body becomes a portable instrument. The body does not disappear in these technological mediations but enables new possibilities for resistance and creates fractures in existing power discourses. Gonçalves (2004) explores these 'strategies of resistance' through an examination of postmodern performance suggesting that during 'mediated' performance the performing body becomes a 'mediatic interface' that can be reconfigured. Gonçalves (2004) also notes that Anderson employs different layers of mediation such as altering her voice electronically to sound like a man's or constructing a hybrid body such as with the suit described above. It does not seem unreasonable to claim that, by incorporating different media and technology into her work, she is able to 'perform resistance from within' (both physically and within the dominant discourses of technology) and that she challenges the 'naturalness' of the female performing body. Anderson's conscious construction of a hybrid technological persona can be seen as deeply political; the control exercised by her in her fusion of body, voice and machine seems to invoke a material 'musical cyborg' that really can reconfigure a technological feminine identity.

Conclusion

In this chapter, I have shown how education policy is increasingly underpinned and informed by a belief that digital technologies are innately democratizing and transformative. There is a belief that all young people, constructed as 'natural' and confident users of technologies, will want and expect to use technology in the classroom, its application in educational settings leading to greater pupil motivation, increased attainment and the raising of standards. I suggested that this mirrors a technological determinist orthodoxy which tends to focus on the technological artefact as having an innate ability to effect change but pays scant attention to the social relations into which that technology is incorporated. Turning to the technologized music classroom, I examined how this determinist trend was reproduced by those championing the use of compositional technologies, and suggested that by neglecting the social aspect of computers and their use means we are unlikely to be aware of the ways in which gendered differences are produced and maintained in the music technology classroom.

Incorporating the social into discussions of technology is crucial otherwise individual agency, resistance and choice are presented as futile in the face of this technological juggernaut. Paying attention to the social nature of technologies acknowledges that the adoption and development of a technology entails making decisions. Williams (1985: 146) is very clear on this point: 'The moment of any new technology is a moment of choice.' Technology is not predetermined, but innovations are related to selections, preferences and choices made by human actors, not mechanical or digital systems. This is not to ignore that power may be implicit in these decisions but it does admit a level of agency that determinist thinking does not accommodate and helps us to understand the ways in which artefacts may be configured, and by whom, in the operation of gender interests. Recognizing that there is nothing inevitable about technology, and that meanings and uses can be redefined, provides 'a more realistic and useful basis for feminist action, precisely because it resonates with the ambivalence that women experience in encounters with technology ... [it] helps to explain the tenacity of the equation between masculinity and technology' (Faulkner, 2001: 80–81), highlighting the dialectical relationship between technology and society. This is a key point helping us to understand why gendered concerns are often marginalized in discourses about music technology, acting as a corrective to determinist perspectives which appear to offer limited possibilities for women to challenge pervasive masculinist music cultures where assumptions about gender serve to position men and women differently in relation to musical activities and musical spaces.

Finally, I looked at how the concept of the 'cyborg' had been appropriated as a way of theorizing women's digital interactions, and its usefulness as a conceptual tool (in the form of a 'musical cyborg)' when examining the issue of female empowerment and agency in women's music practices. There appeared to be an uncritical appropriation of the apparently 'utopian' aspects of the cyborg, which suggests that there is an inevitability about women's assimilation into the technological world. And yet discussions about this human–machine amalgam are more likely to reproduce determinist discourses because the metaphoric cyborg obscures the material social structures that work against the very empowerment that feminists claim technology enables. Consequently, representations of female gendered cyborgs have limited use when arguing for a socially embedded understanding of women's relationship with technology. These symbolic representations do not impact on women's lived experiences as they offer no material challenges to existing oppression, and exclusionary cultures and practices. Unless women themselves have the power to decide upon the nature of these technological unions, applying a cyborgian epithet does nothing to disrupt or dismantle men's material control of music technology and women's bodies within music.

Chapter 3
Gendered Cultures in the Music Technology Classroom

Schools act as key sites in the construction and formation of gender, with teachers playing a key role in policing the boundaries of what constitutes 'appropriate' behaviours and expectations for males and females based on 'common-sense' notions about society and the role of different groups within it. Early studies in gender and education focused on the inequities found in schools that positioned boys and girls differently, often to the detriment of the girls. By revealing this 'hidden curriculum', researchers found that boys often exerted more control over the conversation, interrupted more and often dominated classroom interaction (Spender, 1982; Acker, 1994; Roland Martin, 1994), this 'poor' behaviour often being interpreted by teachers as a sign of boys' greater imagination and creativity compared to that of the quieter, more 'passive' girls (Clarricoates, 1978). The transmission of a 'gender code' (Arnot and Weiner, 1987; Acker, 1994; Arnot, 2002) within the learning experience was said to not only place female pupils at an educational disadvantage but also to reproduce the power relations of the male–female hierarchy, thereby reinforcing and producing conformity to stereotyped gender expectations.

This chapter takes as its starting point the notion that classrooms are established cultures in which teachers and pupils share expectations about the learning settings in terms of what is valued, taught and learned and how this is socially organized (Sheingold et al., 1984). Schooling processes and practices are therefore important in the construction of gender identity, for example, via the gendered ways in which teachers interact with pupils and each other (Francis, 2000; Francis and Skelton, 2001) and via the school curriculum (Paechter, 2000). As Haywood and Mac an Ghaill (2003: 63) state, 'school is a social process, a set of social relations charged with formal and informal meanings. All aspects of schooling are subject to these meanings and they are deployed across a diversity of areas'. Green has studied the role of music education in the reproduction of gendered musical practices, and suggests that teachers and pupils 'collude with each other in the perpetuation of the gender politics of music: the construction of a gendered discourse on music that aids in the regulation of gender' (1997: 186). Describing how gendered ideologies are enacted in the music classroom, Green argues that patriarchal notions of femininity and masculinity remain largely unchallenged, making it difficult for boys and girls to subvert these normative constructions.

The data presented in this chapter explores the processes and practices that produce gendered cultures within the music technology classroom through an examination of the institutional features that frame the educational environment within the four participating schools, presented in Chapter 1. These features include how pupils learn about technology, the repertoire of teacher and pupil talk, its effect on pupil confidence and the issue of male control of technological knowledge. I argue that, while there are differences and similarities in classroom practice within the schools, all produced, to a greater or lesser extent, gendered forms of interaction, types of talk and technological spaces. This suggests that the articulation of technology with masculinity and femininity engenders certain attitudes, forms of interaction and types of classroom organization. As Holloway and Valentine state:

> computers come to mean different things in different schools ... the different ways that these schools have incorporated ICT into their institutional agendas and practices demonstrate that technology has no pre-given effects, but that its meanings and implications emerge as computers and social actors come together ... (Holloway and Valentine, 2003: 42)

This observation is certainly borne out in my discussion of the institutional practices in operation within each school and the meanings each constructs around music technology, and the extent to which pupils learn to take up or, in some cases, resist these institutional practices.

While technological skills learned in school are brought into the home (Holloway and Valentine, 2003), the increasingly media-rich home with its computers, iPods and video games consoles (Livingstone, 2002) means that there is likely to be similar cross-fertilization of technological expertise from home to classroom. As Sefton-Green and Buckingham (1998) note, pupils bring into school a body of knowledge, skills and competencies derived from their out-of-school experiences of computers, and these 'informal' cultural competencies feed into the formal curriculum. As such, the level of engagement, familiarity with digital media and the skills young people develop related to their out-of-school activities will affect their attitudes towards and aptitudes for engaging with music technology and music software in the classroom, and research suggests that this diversity of experience, skills and engagement is highly gendered.

Learning technology

Although research shows there is little difference between boys and girls regarding the presence of computers in the home, boys are more likely to have personal ownership of computers than girls and engage in more frequent use of this technology (Facer et al., 2003). What pupils bring into the classroom is often informed by the types of activities engaged in at home, with girls more likely to use the computer as a word processor for text-based activities or for social networking (BECTA, 2008) while boys make greater use of it for surfing the Net and game-playing (Orr Vered, 1998; Sefton-Green and Buckingham, 1998; Facer et al., 2003; Cranmer, Potter and Selwyn, 2008). Regarding music technology, girls will often use the technology as a tool to help them produce music, but boys were more likely to just play around with it for its own sake (Colley et al., 1997). The authors go on to suggest that this could also be a manifestation of a style of working that reflects boys' and girls' out-of-school experiences with games software. As one teacher from their study commented, 'if there's a knob boys will turn it, if there's a switch they'll press it', while another observed 'it's always the boys that are pressing the buttons on the keyboard ... If you watch them in the keyboard lab they'll be banging away at it, while the girls are actually trying to make music' (1997: 125). Savage and Challis (2002: 14) suggest that technology is an aid to experimentation; learning through playing around, employing an almost 'accidental approach' which facilitates a necessary sense of play and experimentation with technology but, as Colley et al.'s (1997) observations suggest, boys are more likely to adopt a more 'hands-on', 'doodling' approach to working with computers, which is compatible with the types of computer activities they engage with in informal settings. Girls, on the other hand, are less likely to engage with computers in this way, partly because their preferred activities require different types of interactions and because being seen to be interested in computers poses a threat to their femininity.

Girls are more likely to view those who spend large amounts of time using computers as 'geeky' and as not 'having a life', an identity often attributed to boys. Girls assert that they would not tell their peers they were into computers for fear of being seen as a 'sad geek' or a 'boffin' (Holloway and Valentine, 2003). Moreover, the reluctance to be associated with 'geeky' boys can actually reinforce potential anxieties about their level of technological skill when compared to more expert peers, and girls may actively resist using the technology altogether rather than be stigmatized as a technological 'dunce' amongst more competent users. This fear of failure is often one reason given by girls for not using music technology (Comber et al., 1993). Girls, therefore, find themselves in a double bind whereby their feminine identities are at risk if they *do* engage with it and yet, if they do not, they are left feeling inadequate in a classroom culture where knowledge of ICT and technological skill is highly valued. In contrast, ICT reinforces boys' sense of masculine identity, an affirmatory technological identity with which many girls do not feel comfortable.

However, it has been suggested that an overtly technological identity can also be difficult for some boys. Being labelled 'geeky' or 'nerdy' by other pupils, especially by other boys, may be equated with being effeminate or 'poncy' (Holloway and Valentine, 2003) but I could find no examples of this in my findings. In fact, having good technological skills are implicated in the construction of an acceptable and desirable somewhat 'macho' masculinity that is validated by teachers and pupils particularly at Old Tech Grammar, New Tech Comp and, to a lesser extent, Arts College, which Gemma's comments about Robert illustrate:

Gemma: He was taught by someone, I think it was Mr X [now left], and he was taught the sequencers or spent a lesson with Robert and taught him how to do it because he doesn't play an instrument and he spent hours doing one of his compositions … He sequenced it and it was *so* good! He said, his mum timed it over a period of three or four days; he spent pretty much four days solidly working on it. (GCSE girl, Old Tech Grammar)

There is no inference from this account that Robert is considered 'geeky' or 'nerdy'; rather, his ability to work in this way arouses admiration. Gemma's description of Robert's working practices resembles observations made in Hapnes and Sorensen's (1995) study about Norwegian male computer hackers and identity. They argued that a hacker's sense of identity was strongly connected to the high level of competition between hackers who took great pride in setting personal records for how many hours they could spend programming without sleep. As Gemma's description is based on Robert's own account, it is apparent that he is happy to be take on this hacker-type identity secure in the knowledge that, rather than positioning him as 'sad' and needing to 'get a life', his is an identity that inspires respect and admiration amongst his peers.

Acknowledging these different approaches to learning about technology in informal spaces is an important consideration when seeking to understand how pupils engage with and learn about unfamiliar music software packages. This issue was raised in the pupil interviews when they were asked about the extent to which they receive 'formal' training when working with new music software. This is an area largely ignored within discussions of music technology and seems rather remiss if pupils are expected to view the computer 'as a tool for realizing musical ideas' (Folkestad et al., 1998: 94) but may have insufficient knowledge of the range of music software schools expect them to use. Yet this seems to be a common scenario whereby pupils are often expected to engage with music software with only the most rudimentary overview of how to use it: an ad hoc approach to music technology that may be especially detrimental to female composers. A recent BECTA (2008: 13) report noted that 'girls rely on schools to teach them about technology more than boys do – it is therefore clear that schools have an important role to play in giving girls access to technology, providing guidance and support, and employing the appropriate pedagogical strategies to enable boys and girls to use ICT to its full potential'. Some music educators have acknowledged this by providing structured introduction for girls, but this is by no means common practice (Colley et al., 1997).

Asked whether they had been given any structured lessons on how to use the various types of software, it was noticeable that, although many pupils insisted they had received none or very little, this appeared less problematic for the boys, who were more likely to express confidence to try things out anyway. They were more inclined to adopt a 'have a go' approach, expressing less concern when things went wrong, and were more likely to assert that they tended to pick things up as they went along. Given the higher level of computer use amongst boys in the home, this is perhaps not surprising, but it has gendered implications as it has been shown that greater exposure to and experience of using computers is related to more positive computer attitudes (Levine and Donitsa-Schmidt, cited in Colley and Comber, 2003). Gemma's experiences of composition and learning about the basic score-editing software Music Time Deluxe[1] suggests that there is an underlying assumption that pupils already know about the software, or at least can pick up the requisite knowledge as they go along:

> Gemma: Well, I borrowed the Music Time Deluxe software from school. My parents haven't bought it. I think it was in Year 8 I had a different teacher who's left now and he used to go round and, when they first bought the computers and he sort of went round and explained the basics to us but, cos we were in Year 8, we didn't really use them a lot and so now, I can only use Music Time Deluxe and I think a couple of my friends are like that. He [Mr Clarke, Head of Music] talks about the others like Cubase and stuff but we're just not sure how to use them.
> VA: So you've not actually had structured time on sort of 'this is how you do it'?
> Gemma: No, we get sent away and say, they say 'do your compositions' so we [trails off]. Everyone's asking [for help] at the same time. It is quite annoying […] a little more help I suppose is always a good thing. (GCSE girl, Old Tech Grammar)

In contrast, where boys are prepared to acknowledge some degree of formal instruction about inputting notes and so on, they would continue to assert that they could, however, work things out for themselves and seemed to take a certain pride in this ability to display their technological know-how, and this was a strong theme in their responses:

> Edward: Um, well Sibelius I've had for quite a while. My parents bought it for me so I've been using that for a while now and I can do a lot on that but on the MIDI set-up like Cubase, things like that, I mean I've got that at home and use it here but I'm having to teach myself as I go how to use it.
> VA: So when you say you teach yourself as you go, what kind of training were you given to use the equipment at the start of the course?
> Edward: Um, well, like, we weren't given any basic training: 'oh, this is how you …' Well, I suppose you are at the beginning of the school but then, well cos I've got a kind of manual on the computer, so I can look stuff up on that as well, it came with it. (A level boy, Old Tech Grammar)

---

[1]   A simple score editor with some basic sequencing whereby notes are entered via the computer mouse or MIDI keyboard. It is said to be particularly useful for small ensembles and song writing because guitar chords and lyrics can be added to the score.

VA: What kind of training were you given on the software here when you started your course?

Robert: We were told how to use it, how to transpose notes, how to input notes, how to save the documents and all that stuff. I sort of like, I work stuff out as I go along. I find it quite easy to just like find stuff out by myself. I don't read the instruction manuals or anything. (GCSE boy, Old Tech Grammar)

These responses were echoed by Luke at Crossways Independent:

VA: OK. [referring to his questionnaire] You say you feel confident using technology. What do you think you're particularly good at?

Luke: Well, I can hold a mouse! I dunno really. I'm not sure really what you can be good at. It's kind of annoying because a lot of the time it doesn't do what you want it to do but, it has to go a long way around doing something but, um, in general, as long as you've been told what to do you just sit down and do it.

VA: So you don't have any problems?

Luke: No.

VA: Right. So just tell me what kinds of things, how were you taught to use the technology?

Luke: I was just, I dunno. I kind of picked it up myself really. You know, it's fairly easy. I can, I mean I know all of the short cuts, everything now. But no, I mean I can do it really fast. You just sort of learn as you go along.

VA: And what about your classmates? Do you ask any of them if you get stuck?

Luke: No, because I never get stuck at school. (GCSE boy, Crossways Independent)

Luke makes light of how he learns to use the technology. Although it is apparent that he has received some help in how to use the software, evidenced by his statement 'as long as you've been told what to do you just sit down and do it', he downplays this. He is keen to present himself as someone who learns about technology by just picking it up, without apparent effort or concern. As he states, his ability to 'hold a mouse' is sufficient qualification for being 'good' at technology. Robert too acknowledges that he has received some degree of formal instruction but, again, he stresses the ease with which he can work things out for himself and takes a certain pride in his claim that he does not have to resort to using the manual. These boys were keen to portray themselves as competent users who could learn about technology with little formal support. This appearance of 'effortless achievement' (Jackson and Dempster, 2009) belies the formal help and support these boys have received, allowing them to present their technological facility as a result of their innate, natural ability. However, as Gemma observed, even when boys were finding things difficult, they were less inclined to show it:

Gemma: Um, we're [the girls] all about 'ooh, what's going on?' I think the boys
do muck about and if they are struggling they don't show it but we do, but they
don't get their work done in time. (GCSE girl, Old Tech Grammar)

Only a handful of girls across the four schools stated they took a similar approach
to learning about technology, sharing the boys' 'have a go' approach, although
they were happy to state that they would refer to computer manuals if necessary.
Their attitude to 'having a go' seemed for more pragmatic reasons in contrast to
the boys' statements, which appeared to be grounded in their sense of themselves
as competent technologists:

VA: If you have a problem with the technology what do you do?
Lisa: I'll press lots of buttons to see what happens. (GCSE girl, Arts College)

VA: Were you given much training in how to use it, how to do certain things?
Kezia: No, not really. It's pretty straightforward. There used to be a book [the
manual] there so I use that if I get stuck. (GCSE girl, Crossways Independent)

VA: Were you taught how to use the software?
Lyn: Well no. We had a sort of little half hour thing about how to use it at the
start of our course but that's all.
VA: So how did you learn to use it?
Lyn: Well, I look up the help bit and stuff. I usually work it out myself. (A level
girl, Arts College)

These girls were either studying at Arts College or Crossways Independent,
where there appeared to be less emphasis on exhibiting and constructing an overt
technological identity. In contrast to the overtly technological identity encouraged
and prized at Old Tech Grammar and New Tech Comp, girls from Arts College
and Crossways Independent appeared more likely to find ways of reconciling a
positive identity that enabled them to develop a confident and experimental mode
of learning about music technology. This seems of particular significance in light
of the rather curious observation made by Savage and Challis (2002), who point
out that new technologies help develop pupils' creative ideas rather than having to
'worry' about the intricacies of the software:

Whilst in the first instance there was a focus on effective use of software and
hardware, and in developing the necessary technological skills, pupils were
thrown in the creative deep end with some of the technology. They had to sink
or swim with it ... Many rose to the challenge and quickly showed their creative
flair through appropriate uses of the software. (Savage and Challis, 2002: 13)

Much is made of the 'many' but no mention is made of the implied few who were
unable to 'rise to the challenge' of grappling with the software. Not only are we

left in the dark about their ability to show 'creative flair' but we are given no information about their gender either. One can only guess what challenges they faced if they did not have the technological skills to enable them to show their creative flair 'through appropriate uses of the software', nor what happened to those few who sank rather than swam.

This is a significant omission in light of my findings. Although a number of girls stated they were comfortable with the slightly ad hoc approach the schools took to introducing pupils to new music software, these girls were in the minority. Most girls requested more formal training in the use of music software at the beginning of their courses. However, this can play into the hands of gender ideology that equates girls' greater 'need' for more help and reliance on the teacher's guidance with the assumption that they are either less gifted or less able than their male counterparts. These parallels can be found in teachers' attitudes towards boys' and girls' composing, whereby boys' expressed independence from teacher instruction marks them out, in the eyes of their teachers, as being more creative, imaginative and spontaneous than their diligent, unimaginative, conformist female classmates (Green, 1997). The teachers in Green's study acknowledge that girls work harder but state they are more interested in 'getting things right', better at 'exercises' and rather conservative. The boys, on the other hand, are said to have more 'natural ability'; as one teacher noted, 'much of the creative, adventurous composing comes from the boys' (Green, 1997: 197). Consequently, this has important implications given the ways some girls learn to use technology and, despite concerns about the negative gendered perceptions of requiring help, it has been recognized that, in order to increase confidence in their female pupils, it is useful for teachers to provide a structured introduction to new technologies in a step-by-step approach (Colley et al., 1997).

Gendered processes and practices

The remainder of this chapter explores these perceptions further with regard to the production of gendered cultures that both limits girls' involvement in technological practices, and may seriously contribute to many girls' expressed lack of confidence within the music technology classroom. This contrasts with the greater expressions of confidence and feelings of technological control by the boys engendered by an overtly masculine technological discourse produced at Old Tech Grammar, New Tech Comp and marginally less so at Arts College.

Gendered technological talk

'Technological talk' between teachers and pupils and among the pupils themselves contributed to noticeably gendered interactions in the classroom and to the production of a dominant technological discourse that positions males and females differently with regard to technology. Of the four schools, Old Tech Grammar and New Tech Comp represent the extremes of music technology provision: the former had a state-of-the-art music suite that had been in use for a number of years, while New Tech Comp had only a 3:1 pupil–computer ratio and the shortest music technology history of all four schools. Observations at Old Tech Grammar took place in the music technology suite, where a wide range of software was in use. New Tech Comp only invested in technology at the beginning of the academic year in which the research was carried out; until that time, the department had access to only one computer. Throughout the first few classroom observations, I began to discern a marked difference between the schools regarding the amount and type of technological talk that took place in the lessons. This type of talk dominated the classroom interactions with pupils at Old Tech Grammar and New Tech Comprehensive, was less overt at Arts College and was very rare at Crossways Independent. However, it was noticeable that both Old Tech Grammar and New Tech Comprehensive engaged in a technocratic discourse that was oriented towards the perceived interests of the boys, with the male teachers leaving many of the girls positioned outside of the culture generated by these types of discursive practices.

A fifty-minute GCSE composition lesson at New Tech Comprehensive saw pupils scattered about the department: some were in the music room where the majority of the computers were located while others were dotted around the various practice rooms. The class teacher spent the lesson working with any pupil that asked for help in completing their composition coursework, dividing his time between the main music room and three practice rooms (one of which contained a computer). The layout of the main music room was fairly straightforward: twelve electronic keyboards with headphones were arranged on desks around the edges of the room, and towards the front of the classroom, close to the teacher's desk, were three computers. All but one electronic keyboard was in use by female pupils (all working with headphones) so, having noted this I chose to position myself near the front of the room as that was where the majority of male pupils and the teacher were located.

It was noticeable that during this part of the lesson the teacher did not interact with any of the female pupils. He worked with any pupil that required his help but none of the girls requested it. Throughout my observation of this class the boys monopolized the computers, either alone or in groups. They would constantly ask the teacher for help: for example, wanting to know how to put their compositions on to minidisk or how to solve technical problems regarding achieving the correct balance between certain instruments using the sequencing software Cubase VST.[2] At one point, three male pupils working together on one of the computers were trying to solve a problem with one of the boy's compositions as he was unhappy with the sound quality and the 'mix', but they appeared uncertain about how to proceed. The balance of the tracks was incorrect so the teacher showed

---

[2]   This is a MIDI music sequencer which allows the user to edit and record MIDI and audio recording. It acts like a virtual recording studio inside the computer.

the boys how to adjust the volume of each instrument on the track. The majority of interactions I observed between the teacher and the male pupils consisted of 'technological talk' and providing practical help in using the technology which none of the girls participated in.

During this lesson, only one girl worked at a computer; she worked alone and did not ask for help or advice, and it is noteworthy that she was the only girl observed composing using music technology during my observations at New Tech Comprehensive. Due to the ways in which the girls were working (by not demanding attention, or asking for help and generally being quiet), they did not draw the teacher's attention towards them, and neither was my attention drawn towards these girls, for similar reasons. Looking back at my field notes, I can see that my attention was focused on the male pupils' interactions near the front of the class in part due to their 'noisiness' and sheer physical presence; at one point seven boys were clustered around the teacher asking questions. Although the girls were also making use of music technology (the electronic keyboards) I am aware that, in similar ways to the teacher, I was focused on the 'dominant' group of 'technological' boys who were involved in discernible technological interactions and using language related to computers and associated software. This reinforces Faulkner's (2001: 85) observation that the symbolic categorization of technologies as gendered often invokes a hard–soft dualism whereby 'hard' technologies are those deemed to be most powerful whereas the 'soft' technology is smaller scale and mundane. Because the girls did not noticeably participate in any computer oriented ('hard' technology) technological talk, I too, like the teacher, rendered them largely invisible and was culpable in their construction as 'non-technologists' because they were 'only' using electronic keyboards ('soft' technology). This will be explored further in Chapter 5, but the above serves to demonstrate how easily girls' technological involvement can be obscured and disregarded when boys are allowed to monopolize teacher time and talk.

Observations at Old Tech Grammar also highlighted how the majority of teacher–pupil interactions involved technologically focused discussions, which rarely involved female pupils. During my first GCSE observation at the school, the pupils began the lesson in the main music room where each pupil was seated in front of an electronic keyboard. Having taken the register, the teacher instructed the pupils to continue working on their coursework composition assignments and sent them into the music ICT suite next door. The teacher was largely absent throughout the remainder of the lesson as he was busy trying to organize the rehearsal and performance schedule for the Year 11's GCSE practical performance exam. Another male teacher entered the room briefly and one of the boys asked him a technical question, but the teacher instructed him to 'read the manual' and then left the room. On subsequent visits to this particular timetabled class, the designated teacher, Mr Clarke, was present and I became aware that he spent a significant amount of time talking about the hardware/software aspects of technology. The suite was quite an informal space with pupils moving around freely, and with A level pupils also coming in and out during the lessons. During the second GCSE observation, two male A level pupils entered the suite and began talking to the teacher about problems of 'overdubbing' using the multi-track in the adjacent recording studio. Mr Clarke dealt with this enquiry and then engaged in two further discussions, one about recording onto a minidisk player and another about transferring music files to floppy disc, all with male pupils. All these technologically oriented interactions were with male pupils, interactions that illustrate the ways in which the structural and symbolic associations between masculinity and technology are played out in educational settings. As Faulkner (2001) observes, men often have greater success at claiming skill status and technological competence, and this can have the effect of rendering invisible or insignificant women's contributions to technological interactions and claims for technological competence. It is difficult to assess the extent to which the girls' exclusion from these technological interactions was a result of their 'alienation' from this technocratic masculine culture (Turkle, 1984), or their ambivalence towards the technology (Cooper, 2007), and perhaps such a stark division should not be made. As Abbis (2008: 162) rightly notes, we must be careful of locating the 'problem' of technological participation as simply about the construction of male computer cultures, arguing that 'there would be no problem if the tendency to privilege male practice were undermined', but Abbis goes on to say that this is unlikely 'given the potency of the symbolic association of masculinity with technology'. The scenarios depicted above are powerful examples of the tenacity of this association and how it continues to be played out by male teachers and pupils in technological spaces.

Similarly, the above discussion reflects Culley's (1988) observations regarding the difficulties of deconstructing a gendered technological discourse when men have more power than women to define and circumscribe talk and interactions. In her study of secondary school computer clubs Culley found that fewer girls than boys took part in these optional activities. The computer rooms were generally thought of as 'male' territory, the girls stating that the boys' attitudes and behaviours often made them feel uncomfortable. To compensate, schools provided 'girls-only' time (often supervised by a non-specialist female teacher), but this led to the open sessions effectively becoming boys-only sessions (run by a qualified male computer teacher) which had the effect of further reducing access and teaching quality for the girls. The above reflects what many researchers have found: boys frequently get more attention and occupy more of the teacher's time. Lesson content and discussion are geared towards boys in order to deal with their greater demand for attention and social control (Spender, 1982; Acker, 1994) and this is further compounded when technology becomes the focus of classroom interactions.

In a recent Ofsted report (2001, cited in Warren, 2003) it was noted that boys were doing less well in science (attributed to their relative weakness in basic communication skills), leading Ofsted to propose significant changes to the curriculum and teaching strategies to address this. It suggested that in order to draw out boys' 'natural ability' greater use of ICT was required in literacy work and more 'instrumental' uses to support writing should be adopted rather than focusing on 'expressive' forms. Warren (2003: 205) argues this invokes what he calls 'particular ideas of masculine practice in more "active" forms of pedagogy' or more prosaically 'boy-friendly' methods which produce 'a dichotomous distinction between the "instrumental" male and the "expressive" female' (2003: 205). Unfortunately, such common-sense views of gender differences can lead to an uncritical adoption of 'appropriate' teaching methods for boys and girls. This is a worrying turn and reinforces the concern expressed by Skelton and Francis (2009: 137) that 'interventions based on constructed gender divisions, which were worked against and broadly eradicated in the late 1980s and early '90s ... now seem to be making a comeback' (Skelton and Francis, 2009: 137). These simplistic notions of gendered learning styles are problematically rendered as 'tips for teachers', as exemplified by Baldock's (2009) use of an Australian music programme called 'Boys' Business' to encourage boys' participation in education (Smith, 2004,) which is

> built on the premise that all boys have an 'inner wild man', a natural aggressor with a survival instinct. Boys don't like to be confronted; it awakens their wild man and can accelerate to conflict unnecessarily. They go into survival mode, and the 'fight or flight' instinct engages. Angry or reluctant boys are not engaged learners ... (Baldock, 2009: 96)

This alarmingly essentializing account of boys results in eleven 'tips for working with boys' compared to only five for working with girls, from which one can infer that they are perceived as more amenable, less boisterous and more easily engaged in the music classroom. What is particularly problematic is that 'tips for working with boys' include advice for teachers to be creative, a risk taker, friendly, positive, patient, willing to smile and laugh but these 'tips' are not included for working with girls. However, working with girls (but not boys) includes the instruction to be 'expectant of high academic achievement, participation and social maturity' (Baldock, 2009: 102) reinforcing notions of femininity as well behaved, grown up and serious. This only serves to reinforce stereotypical views about the differences between males and females, differences that produce and maintain unequal power relationships that focus on the needs and interests of male pupils.

Confidence and control

Having highlighted how male pupils and teachers can dominate and control technological talk in the classroom, the following examines how this impacts on the varying levels of technological confidence expressed by boys and girls within the schools. The powerful technocratic discourses produced at Old Tech Grammar and New Tech Comprehensive appear to be a significant contributory factor for girls' expressed lower levels of confidence within these two schools. In addition, it appears that these male-dominated technological interactions contribute to spaces that are not comfortable for girls. Due to their limited access to the technological language involved in these interactions – which, as I suggested above, contribute to gendered classroom cultures – girls may find themselves positioned *outside* the culture generated by the male teachers and male pupils, creating an environment which results in girls being unable or unwilling to contribute to these technological discourses.

Wajcman (1991) has suggested that women attach different meanings and values to technology, and that these enter into our understanding and construction of gendered identities. Masculinity is constructed through notions of technical competence, while the idea that women lack this technical competence becomes part of a feminine gendered identity. Henwood (1993) argues not only that levels of competence and confidence relate to how pupils acquire technical skills but also that they must own that acquisition at a more subjective level, as part of their overall identities. However, this 'ownership' of technical skills is inhibited by their exposure to constructions of gender–technology relations that posit women as 'outsiders' within technological cultures, as the previous discussion regarding 'technological talk' highlighted. Computers are not inherently gendered, but they are said to be more attractive to boys because computer culture is more consistent with traditional types of male activities (Kiesler et al., 1985; Sofia, 1998), a culture that may repel girls. This seems credible in light of Ofsted's (2009) recent evaluation of secondary school music, which showed that five times more boys than girls opt for music technology courses. Turkle believes that women are not phobic about computers but 'reticent' because the computer becomes a 'personal and culture symbol of what a woman is not' (1988: 41).

Therefore, it is crucial that we examine the cultural landscape in which computer use occurs to enable us to better understand how it shapes our understanding of what computing 'means'. Huber and Schofield's (1998) research into computer use in Costa Rican primary schools exemplifies this point. They observed that the teaching within these schools was heavily gender-stereotyped whereby males were expected to excel intellectually and were allowed to dominate social relationships within the classroom while girls, on the other hand, were expected to be submissive, pious, decent and more interested in spiritual and moral matters in preparation for their social role as housewives and mothers (over 75 per cent of Costa Rican women do not work outside the home). They suggest that these cultural expectations reflect children's attitudes to computers: boys were much more enthusiastic about computer technology while girls, in comparison, appeared less confident and were less likely to use them during non-teaching time. These observations show how the meanings created around computer technology reflect cultural expectations: males and females are educated with different social roles in mind, which, in turn, legitimate differential expectations of their intellectual capabilities, behaviours and gendered subject positions.

Colley and Comber (2003) also report that boys are more confident users of technology than girls and that girls are more likely to underestimate their computing ability in relation to others; girls are also more likely to report greater feelings of incompetence with computers than males (Schumacher and Morahan-Martin, 2001). Boys show higher levels of self-assurance, and there is a *perception* amongst boys and girls that boys generally know what they are doing, reinforcing a cultural stereotype of the competent male computer user (Comber et al., 1993; Colley et al., 1997) a perception that was evident from the pupil responses in my study. During their interviews, when asked whether they thought there was a difference between boys' and girls' ability to use music technology, the responses were overwhelmingly in favour of the boys:

> Robert: I think it's the boys who are better at using the technology in our class. I don't know why. The girls seem to always wonder how to do stuff. Like [female pupil], she doesn't even know how to put the floppy disk in the drive to make it work properly. She must be like not computer literate. (GCSE boy, Old Tech Grammar)

> Steve: Um, I think there is possibly a bit less on the girls' side cos they ain't used it as much like me and Robert. So I don't think it's just cos they're girls. (GCSE boy, Old Tech Grammar)

> Craig: It's probably the boys, most of the boys. Not all of them but, on average, they would be better musically in our class because we've got two sequencers and none of the girls are sequencers. Maybe the boys are a bit better at using computers and musically. (A level boy, Old Tech Grammar)

> Karen: Boys, probably because I think Luke's the best. Yeah, generally the boys. (GCSE girl, Crossways Independent)

> Ian: Well, I'd actually say the boys because Karen doesn't really use it and there's only Kezia. She's good and Luke's good and Harry as well, so I'd say the boys. I don't know [hesitates] it's kind of hard because it's 50–50 really. So I don't really like want to say the boys or girls but if I had to choose one I'd have to choose the boys. (GCSE boy, Crossways Independent)

Currently there is little agreement about the issue of gender and confidence around music technologies. One study carried out into the use of ICT in the Scottish music curriculum stated that the teachers did not perceive any gender differences regarding levels of confidence, although they note that the use of technology had increased access to music education for boys far more than for girls (Byrne and Macdonald, 2002), an observation supported by other studies (Colley et al., 1993; Ofsted, 2009). However, it is important to point out that just because teachers did not notice any gender differentiation there were no gender differences. Byrne and Macdonald's (2002) study was carried out using only teacher focus groups so it is difficult to substantiate teachers' assertions that gender was not an issue without supporting evidence gleaned from their actual classroom practice. Gendered attitudes towards information technology use in music classrooms in Hong Kong (Ho, 2004) also suggest little difference between boys' and girls' levels of confidence and interest. Consistent with other studies, however, was the observation that there were more positive responses for music technology from the primary school girls than from secondary school girls. Colley and Comber (2003), in their study of age and gender differences in computer use in secondary schools, also found that younger pupils reported a greater liking for computers while older girls tended to compare their computing ability less favourably with boys of the same age than the younger groups.

Pitts and Kwami (2002) also note little of the antipathy that had been expected in light of other research towards girls' use of music technology (Armstrong, 1999, 2001), but somewhat problematically skate over what seems a highly significant point when they note that one female pupil was 'particularly disillusioned with the ICT process, preferring the immediacy of the piano and its almost physical contact with the player to the virtual world of the MIDI keyboard' (2002: 67). I will return to this important aspect of computer-mediated composition in Chapter 7 for a full exposition of its significance but, suffice to say, this pupil's comment hints at unexplored gender issues. As I have suggested elsewhere, it is not necessarily antipathy towards music technology but towards a *style* or *mode* of compositional process. It is the technological focus and emphasis on technological control to which girls are reacting (Armstrong, 2001: 37). As such, the observation made by Pitts and Kwami (2002) may say less about the pupils' attitudes towards music technology and more about the culture and organizational arrangements of the classroom which I have argued in this chapter are key to understanding gender–technology relations.

In comparison to some of the studies discussed above my findings are significantly different. Once the results from the eighty-one completed questionnaires (thirty-nine girls and forty-two boys) were collated, it was significant that the question 'Do you feel confident using music technology for composing?' elicited 'yes' from 90 per cent of the boys compared to only 48 per cent of the girls. It was also interesting to note that the lowest levels of confidence were expressed by girls from Old Tech Grammar, which had the best equipped music technology suite and unlimited access to the equipment – lack of access being one of the reasons often given for girls' lower levels of interest. As Colley et al (1997: 126) note, school type significantly influences the confidence of female pupils when working with music technology. Many of the girls felt unconfident using the technology, stating that it was complicated and unpredictable:

VA: Now, the first thing is you say [on your questionnaire] that you don't feel very confident using this stuff. Why is that?
Nina: It's complicated and it mucks you about sometimes. If you do the slightest thing wrong it will close down and not say where your work is.
VA: Did you have a lot of tuition before you starting using it?

Nina: No. Just sort of like straight on there. So, it is a bit difficult to use at first but you get used to it but it's all the little things. You've got to do specific commands for each thing and it's quite difficult finding them because we don't get given the instruction booklet. It's like, 'There's Sibelius, get on with it.'
VA: Right, so you have to use help functions and things like that?
Nina: Yeah. We'll just go through all the menus. Cos sometimes the help functions just sort of like drive you round in circles. They don't really answer your question so we have to figure it out for ourselves. (A level girl, Old Tech Grammar)

Gemma: Because you can play it into the software but it's just the rhythm is very rigid in the software and if you just veer off the rhythm a bit it goes completely wrong and comes out completely wrong note values and it looks horrible and you think 'Oh my God, what have I done here?' (GCSE girl, Old Tech Grammar)

Carolyn: I'm sort of confident but I still find areas where other people would be off and away where I'm still not quite certain of myself. But I think because it's a whole new thing to me. I've had a bit of a problem with the layout of one of my compositions just because, don't know why, I put a guitar line right at the beginning of the instruments I was going to use and once, I deleted it completely. It threw all the, well, it's now got very big gaps between some [notes] and others are very close together on the page and it looks slightly odd.
VA: No obvious reason why that happened?
Carolyn: No and I can't figure out how to change it. (A level girl, Crossways Independent)

On the questionnaire pupils were asked to suggest what might help them gain confidence in using music technology, and large numbers of girls made comments such as 'having instructions available at school', 'Tuition. How to use the different programmes, what effects can be achieved' or just 'Having a manual to look at', comments which reflect the observations I made earlier regarding girls' approaches to learning about technology.

These interview comments contrasted sharply with the male pupils, who expressed a high degree of confidence in their ability to engage with technology, often emphasizing its 'simplicity':

Craig: I'm quite confident at most of it. I find it quite easy to pick up a new piece of software and start using it. Um, because I enjoy it as I'm probably better. I am, I think, fairly able to do most things. (A level boy, Old Tech Grammar)

VA: Now, who's the best person in the class at using the technology?
Robert: Me!
VA: So what do you think you're particularly good at?

Robert: I'm just good at computing in general. I'm trying to create my own video game at the moment. I'm just computer literate. Is that how you say it? [...]

VA: If you do get stuck... do you ever get stuck?

Robert: Um, not now. Maybe in Year 9 I might have got stuck once or twice. We only just got the computers then so I didn't know anything about them at that time but now I literally know how to do most things.

VA: Do you ever ask for help?

Robert: I work it out myself. (GCSE boy, Old Tech Grammar)

VA: You say [from the questionnaire] that you feel confident using technology.

Paul: Yeah, like playing in the notes and stuff; that's about it really. (A level boy, New Tech Comprehensive)

Patrick: Well, it's simple to use. It's got all the sounds, any sound you want. (GCSE boy, New Tech Comprehensive)

Issues of confidence and control of technology are not evident from the male pupils' comments in contrast to those made by Nina, who stated that the smallest mistake can lead to work being lost, and she evinces a lack of control over what the computer does: 'it' (the computer) closes down and then will not 'say' where the work has gone. In addition, Nina's articulation of lack of confidence is compounded by the fact that she has limited knowledge about the software help functions; a situation also experienced by Carolyn at Crossways Independent. Valentine and Holloway (2001: 7) cite a similar example by two of their female respondents, who recount how a girl on one of the respondent's work experience placement accidentally wiped off some important data from a computer merely by pressing 'a button with her little finger' and that 'it just wiped everything'. They suggest that this implies a lack of responsibility for the loss of the document attributing blame to 'it' (the computer) for its loss. Girls' reluctance to engage with technology is not just about having the confidence to 'control' the computer but also demonstrates fears 'that the technology itself might have the power to undermine them' (Valentine and Holloway, 2001: 66). This fear of 'mak[ing] a mess of things' was also evident from Comber et al.'s (1993) female respondents. The boys above express no such concerns, stating they were confident about their abilities to manipulate and control the computer, either attributing this to natural ability at being 'good at computing' or playing down that there might be anything difficult about using computers. This aspect of both being *in* control and being able *to* control the technology is an important element in the boys' constructions of themselves as confident ICT users.

This reinforces Wajcman's (1991) point regarding how either having or lacking technical competence is constituted in gendered identities. Gendered expectations of women working in areas of popular music that require technological competence can make it difficult for women to take ownership of their technological skills, and for this to become a valued part of their professional and gendered identity. For women mix engineers in the popular music industry the manipulation of sound involves issues of power and control on a material level because they are inherent in dictating who has access to the technology (Sandstrom, 2000). Men often dominate the production of music and control the field of sound and recording. Therefore, when women do enter this male domain the gender of the person who mixes the sound becomes an issue of control, as it is not normally women who are in control of these technologies (or the male performers whose music they mix). Consequently, female DJs and sound engineers can find it difficult establishing professional credibility and technical aptitude when doing 'men's work' (Smaill, 2005).

As males continue to dominate technological domains, through the coupling of technology with masculine notions of expertise, rationality and mental logic, it becomes apparent that this production of a masculine discourse of technology in the music classroom helps boys to position themselves positively in relation to technology whilst preventing girls from achieving a similar level of affirmation. Caputo (1994: 88) believes this connection between technology and 'malestream', rational, androcentric ways of knowing reinforces the role of computer technology as a tool for allowing pupil musicians to 'gain control' of the sound through manipulation; music technology shifts attention away from creativity, now emphasizing the notion of 'control'. This with be explored in more detail in Chapter 6.

Sharing technological knowledge and power

Sharing technological knowledge is an important element in men's production of a technological masculinity: not only having control of the technology but also being the arbiters of technological knowledge and having the power to decide with whom to share that knowledge. Often, within technological settings, females are perceived as being the beneficiaries of male technological know-how rather than the dispensers. Within my study, this situation was palpable from the pupils' comments:

> Edward: Out of the girls, there's three doing music. A couple of times they've not known how to do something so I've shown them if Sir isn't around. (A level boy, Old Tech Grammar)

> VA: So do you ask Edward for help?
> Nina: Um, not really. I go to the teachers.
> VA: Right. You don't ask anyone else in your class?
> Nina: Well, I usually ask Chloe because she's quite good at it and she's more approachable than Edward. (A level girl, Old Tech Grammar)

Gemma: And also there are a few people in our class who are better, who are really good but they'll be like 'No, I'm not helping you, I've done mine'. Ya know, they're a bit [trails off]
VA: Who would that be?
Gemma: Robert, right. He's the main one. He's got the knowledge but he won't share it. (GCSE girl, Old Tech Grammar)

Despite Edward's assertion that the girls in his class would turn to him for help this was not borne out by Nina's comment that she would ask a more 'approachable' female member of the class. Even when help was requested, the boys refused, an observation made by other researchers (Facer et al., 2003). Bayton's (1998) study of women pop musicians indicates that this scenario is quite common within the masculinist culture of the recording studio. Technical knowledge and 'techno-jargon' used by the predominantly male studio technicians is not shared with women technicians, as Roberta's comments illustrate:

Sound technology is controlled by men and a lot of men want to keep it to themselves. They don't take you seriously as a woman. Some men are fine but the situation is generally that you are liable, as a woman, to be given wrong information, misleading information. They're so possessive about it. Or, they just won't let you near it. (Female respondent, cited in Bayton, 1998: 7)

This mirrors the situation observed by Feldberg and Glenn (1983) in a customer service department for a US utility company. Initially, men had dominated this type of work, having originally been service engineers who had worked their way up the ranks. As computer technology became central to customer services, the organization of labour saw a shift from a predominantly male to a predominantly female workforce. Even though male and female clerks were doing the same job, men's greater knowledge of the physical environment was used to imbue their work with higher status. This 'special knowledge', reinforced by cultural assumptions that males are more authoritative, contributed to men becoming 'informal consultants' to the women, with the men viewing themselves as experts who 'help the girls out' despite the fact that the work was the same for both. Through not only emphasizing the appearance of having technical know-how but exercising *power* over whom to share it with, these men, and the boys within this study, are constructing a masculine identity that is bound up in traditional concepts of what it means to be male. The cultural stereotype of science and technology, for example, as tough and rational offers masculinity 'something' particularly important (Harding, 1986), where definitions of skill and technological know-how maintain notions about men and masculinity. Therefore, feminists argue, the definition of skill is used as a political concept that perpetuates power relations between men and women. The girls' experiences of having the boys' supposedly greater ICT knowledge and skill withheld from them shows how these power relations are also played out within the classroom between male and female pupils.

When played out between teachers and pupils, these power relations can have a devastating effect. At Old Tech Grammar, in particular, there was an expectation that, as high academic achievers, pupils were capable of working things out for themselves, both technologically and musically. Mr Clarke, the Head of Department at Old Tech Grammar, would often refer to the pupils in his GCSE class as all 'A stars' (the highest grade achievable at GCSE) and made a point of omitting questions in a revision class on African drumming as 'too easy for you', stating that he wanted to give them nothing less than 'A standard questions at this level'. However, as Gemma's comments indicate, not all pupils were equipped with the requisite technical or musical knowledge to meet these high expectations. Although I did not witness the following exchange, Gemma's perception of how these expectations are enacted in classroom encounters is illuminating:

> Gemma: Miss Prime, we have her on Thursdays and she's really helpful cos she will actually explain to us how to do things with computers but Mr Clarke [Head of Department] just kind of presumes we're all A star standard. I don't want to bitch about a teacher but he's really musical and he seems to think that everyone else can just do it like that. Mmm, it's like [female pupil] can't read music; I think she's beginning to now but at the beginning of Year 10 she definitely couldn't and she explained to Mr Clarke and he said 'That's just ridiculous'. He never actually said 'Oh, I'll teach you how to read it'. He just told her she was basically stupid. We're still helping her in class. Like if he says 'Use this scale', she's like 'what's the scale of G major?' So she's never actually been taught it.
> VA: So he makes assumptions about where you should all be when you come into Year 10. I suppose because a lot of you play …
> Gemma: Yeah, but we're all different standards so, I mean you've got some people who are like Grade 8 on three different instruments and some of us are more, y'know … (GCSE girl, Old Tech Grammar)

This is an example of the power-differential between a male teacher and a female pupil and produced a situation in which the GCSE girls rarely asked the teacher for help, preferring to draw upon their friendship networks for advice in the music technology suite. My findings suggest that this situation was a major contributory factor to the macho technological culture that was evident at Old Tech Grammar as Gemma's earlier comment about Robert's refusal to share his knowledge also illustrates. In their work on masculinities, Haywood and Mac an Ghaill (2003) suggest that teacher identities provide an important context for the formation of masculine subjectivities and they have a central role in dictating curriculum choices and producing hierarchically organized knowledges which represent an institutionalized gendered regime. The teacher's unwillingness to take the female pupil's comments at face value and his subsequent withholding of the 'technical' information of music theory is a powerful example of how important the role of the teacher remains in both the symbolic and material construction of the classroom culture.

Conclusion

This chapter has outlined the ways in which gendered practices and processes contribute to the construction of the cultural context in which pupils are expected to compose with music technology. Where boys make use of music technology at home their knowledge, when transferred into the classroom, appears to be accorded value. This feeds back into the masculine culture of a setting that appears not to accord similar status to girls' technological expertise, further strengthening the construction of masculinity as aligned with knowledge, power and culture. Having highlighted gendered differences in boys' and girls' approaches to learning about computers and music software I demonstrated how differences in levels of confidence between boys and girls could be seen as products of an overtly technocratic discourse that was produced and dominated by the males in the classroom.

Throughout, I have emphasized that this is not to suggest that girls cannot use technology or are less interested in it but that they are more likely to express lower levels of confidence and greater anxiety about what it means to 'control' it. This is in direct contrast to the boys' appearance of greater self-assurance when learning and talking about technology, and they are more likely to position themselves as the main arbiters and controllers of technological knowledge. Girls expressed lower levels of confidence in their use of music technology, which indicates that, despite the rhetoric of 'widening access' supporting the push for greater levels of ICT in schools, the availability of computers alone is not the only issue in promoting educational equity. As feminist technology initiatives unfortunately indicate, merely arguing for the widening of women's access to ICT falls some way short of addressing more deep-seated reasons for many women's absence from and ambivalence towards computer technology. Greater numbers of women in technology-based occupations do not automatically lead to a change in either the culture or the structures of an organization. Even where women achieve powerful positions in which they may materially effect change, they seldom do. In her discussion of female scientists Harding (1991) argues that they are often 'complicitous with male domination' in that they do not tackle such issues as the domination of other women from different classes and races, and, ultimately, the structures that produce hierarchical relations remain intact.

A strong theme throughout this chapter has been to show how male teachers and male pupils appear to have more power to actively produce gendered technological cultures, which positions female pupils in a marginalized role that stands outside of the male-produced culture. I showed that there was a palpable difference in levels of confidence at Crossways Independent and Arts College, where far higher numbers of girls overall expressed that they were confident about using music technology. The teachers at these two schools were more circumspect about their technological abilities and they would often elicit advice from the pupils about technological problems; a situation I never witnessed at Old Tech Grammar or New Tech Comprehensive. The overtly gendered discourse of technology produced by the teachers at Old Tech Grammar and New Tech Comprehensive left many girls stating they felt unconfident about their technological abilities, and there appeared to be little room for resistance or renegotiation within these classroom cultures.

Chapter 4
Gendering Technological Expertise

Having highlighted the ways male teachers and pupils dominate technological talk and control technological knowledge, this chapter specifically addresses teachers' and pupils' perceptions of expertise in the classroom focusing on two areas: the construction of the 'technological expert' and the gendering of music software. As feminist STS perspectives show the alignment of men and masculinity with technology are strongly associated with notions of control, power and skill and in the following I explore how these symbolic connections are also played out in the way music software packages become associated with masculinity and femininity. The more 'expertise' required to manipulate the software, the more status is conferred upon those who use it. When music software is perceived to be complicated and difficult boys are more likely to want to engage with it and these types of software are more likely to be viewed as a 'masculine' technology. On the other hand, when music software is regarded as simple and easy to use, the meanings ascribed to it are significantly altered for male users because it offers little symbolic affirmation of a technological masculine identity; the perception of simplicity contributes to its construction as a feminine technology.

Gendering technological expertise and skill

It has been suggested that an important aspect of a successful masculine identity is through the use of powerful technologies and machines (Cockburn, 1985). Within the workplace, masculinity and work have traditionally been defined through a form of skilled labour requiring 'special knowledge' but, as technology continues to develop, machines simplify and more narrowly circumscribe the nature of the occupations into which they are introduced, which may in turn lead to the deskilling and degradation of the work that men do. Henwood et al. (2000) make the important point that skill is not a gender-neutral term, but underpins the socially constructed nature of gender–technology discourses which contribute to the binary opposition of masculine/technical and feminine/non-technical (Henwood et al., 2000: 116). Within the computer industry, the least technical jobs are often occupied by women and they are more likely to be involved in data entry than as programmers or systems analysts (Strober and Arnold, cited in Henwood, 1993: 32). Wajcman (1991: 89) states that 'men's relationship to technology is defined differently to women's … Machines are extensions of male power and signal men's control over the environment.' Men are said to derive different meanings from their work and may therefore feel affronted when they have to do 'women's work', as this is seen as degrading and reduced in status. It is notable that despite men's apparent need to 'control' technology they readily relinquish control of simple 'feminine' domestic technologies (Wajcman, 1991; Kirkup et al., 1992; Cockburn and Furst Dilic, 1994) because they are not affirmatory of a masculine identity predicated on skill and technological expertise. Domestic 'white goods' such as washing machines and cookers become associated with 'feminine' technologies, technologies used for routine tasks that women do every day rather than those non-routine tasks that men so often undertake (Faulkner, 2001). For example, to reduce its feminine connotations and to encourage men's use of this domestic appliance, the microwave oven was initially presented as a technologically interesting 'pie-warmer' rather than as an appliance for home cooking (Ormrod, 1994) and, as such, would not be seen as challenging stereotyped notions of masculinity. As Wajcman (2004: 112) observes, 'in contemporary Western society, the hegemonic form of masculinity is still associated with technical prowess and power. Feminine identity ... has involved being ill-suited to technological pursuits.' The technological artefact in the domestic setting has little value attached to it; therefore, as a benchmark of masculinity there is little kudos or power attached to using a washing machine.

As initially outlined in Chapter 1, a similar ideology is played out in relation to music composition whereby the type of knowledge and skills required to compose 'implies a masculine delineation of mind ... the more that technology is involved, the more masculine the delineation is, and conversely, the less that technology is involved, the less masculine the delineation is' (Green, 1997: 193). Having control of compositional technique and 'technical know-how' further contributes to these delineations. Male composers are the doers and creators of large-scale works, works that require significant technical knowledge of instrumentation and compositional technique. Women, on the other hand, are historically associated with small-scale forms (such as songs and works for solo instruments) intended for relatively private, domestic performance outlets, and these are considered not to require such extensive technical knowledge. Therefore, 'the more vocal, the less technologically informed the compositional process is; and the more instrumental, orchestral or electronic, the more technologically informed it is' (Green, 1997: 84). The more technology is involved, the more masculine the delineation, thus large-scale forms are potentially prohibitive to women. This leads Green to conclude that the less technologically demanding smaller-scale musical forms are unlikely to conflict with patriarchal constructions of femininity and are acceptable compositional forms for women composers. Both technical and technological expertise are thereby associated with the cerebral and become benchmarks of male identity.

The construction of male technological expertise can therefore be said to emanate from this hierarchical gender relationship that sees masculinity and femininity as oppositional and in which the connection between technology and masculinity affords men greater control and power in circumscribing 'who counts' and 'what counts' in technological spaces. This reinforces the conviction that masculinity is allied to notions of technical competence, whereas women's apparent 'lack' of technical competence becomes part of a type of feminine gender identity that is expected of women (Wajcman, 1991). As McNeil (1987) points out, arguing for a 'feminist' technology that resists male expertise is not possible because women are inescapably part of the cultural setting. Turkle and Papert (1990) believe that the new computer culture is about creating not just new environments but a new social construction of the computer. By this they mean forging new ways of thinking about what computing 'means' in order to encompass and embrace all subjective experiences and meanings. In a technological environment, who is supposed to be good at using technology or take part in it is often determined by cultural assumptions about technology (Grint and Gill, 1995). As such, the definition of skill can be used as a political concept that perpetuates power relations between men and women.

Gendering technological skill and expertise in the music classroom

Having considered how skill and expertise become symbolically associated with masculinity, drawing on classroom observation can help us to understand how such meanings are materially and symbolically constructed in the music classroom. The gendered division of labour (both real and perceived) between male and female teachers has a significant impact on how pupils view teachers' technological competence. In turn, these constructions also serve to restrict which pupils have the title of technological expert conferred upon them, with boys significantly more likely to be accorded such status.

The teacher as technological expert

There is a notable absence of references to the teacher within government ICT policy documents other than as a person who must implement and integrate new ICTs into the classroom to improve teaching and learning. Teachers themselves are not conceptualized as individuals who also negotiate and contribute to the gendered space of the digital classroom. In their work on teachers' working identities and new technology, Jenson and Brushwood-Rose (2003) noted that very few women in their case study schools held technical computing or even support positions. The IT specialist was usually a male member of staff, with most of the computer labs taught and overseen by a male teacher, who was referred to as the 'technical person'. Drawing on the experiences of one female teacher, a computer-literate and highly skilled member of a three-person technology team, the authors found that this female teacher was largely relegated to support roles by both her team members and other staff members, a position she found very difficult to counteract even though she was equally well qualified in ICT and had comparable experience to her two male colleagues. Subsequent interviews with teachers in the school indicated that when problems arose they would generally ask advice from the two male co-workers, whom they were happy to label as 'experts'. The female team member was never named as a technology expert by her colleagues, a position that was quite contrary to her level of knowledge and expertise.

Classroom observations in this study revealed that similar constructions of male expertise can also be found in the music technology classroom, and this was particularly noticeable at New Tech Comprehensive and Old Tech Grammar, where male teachers are constructed as the main arbiters of technological knowledge. Mr Graham, Head of Music at New Tech Comprehensive, was always available to resolve technical problems and worked on an ad hoc basis with the pupils as and when they called upon his assistance (which was often). During his interview I asked him if all members of staff were familiar with using music technology. He said that he and another male member of staff were familiar with it but the other (female) member of staff was not. In an informal conversation with the female member of staff I discovered that she had not received any specific music technology training upon appointment. Having been out of classroom teaching for thirteen years she felt that she was 'learning from the pupils ... they know far more than me. I just let them get on with it.' Not surprisingly, during classroom observations male teachers were perceived as the main source of technological information and the key 'troubleshooters' for ICT problems.

This construction of the male teacher as expert was also strong in the music department at Old Tech Grammar, which consisted of two male teachers and one female teacher all of whom taught GCSE and A level. In my interview with Miss Prime she told me this was her second post since qualifying and that although she was still quite new to music technology she stated that she was a confident user and had no real concerns about engaging with it. The Head of Department, Mr Clarke, was, by his own account, *the* technical expert. When asked who sorted out problems in the technology suite he replied 'Me, always me'. The third teacher, Mr Smith, had a very confident manner in the music technology suite although I never actually observed him teaching (and so he was not formally interviewed). This *appearance* of confidence around technology, however, belied some observable limitations in his actual knowledge, but the way he dealt with this during an encounter with Miss Prime illustrates how Mr Smith actively constructed himself as an expert, not just through his mode of social interaction but through his physical control of the computer and the surrounding space. This occurred during an A level composition class in the music technology suite where pupils were working individually at their workstations. Mr Smith entered the room and immediately engaged Miss Prime in conversation. He wanted to set passwords for the computers so that the screensaver could not be changed, thereby preventing pupils 'messing about' with them during lessons. Miss Prime told Mr Smith that she did not know how to do this and he admitted neither did he but that he would try to sort it out. He promptly sat in front of one of the computers immediately placing his hand on the mouse, while Miss Prime sat on a chair to the left of him giving the appearance that they would work on this task together as neither of them had done it before. Mr Smith then spent about ten minutes playing around with various possibilities and eventually found out how to set the password so that the screensaver could not be changed. Throughout the duration of this task he neither spoke to nor acknowledged the female colleague sitting next to him. This resulted in her having no physical control over the computer; nor was her advice sought to rectify this minor technological dilemma. Although both teachers admitted they did not know how to solve the problem, the male teacher, by physically controlling the space around the computer and not engaging verbally with the female teacher, outwardly gave the appearance (to others in the room) of knowing what he was doing. This allowed the male teacher to actively construct himself as the technological expert, an identity not equally available to the female teacher in this scenario.

During the interviews I asked pupils, some of whom had been in the technology suite at the time of the above encounter, if they thought there were any differences between their teachers in terms of their ability to use music technology. From their comments, Miss Prime was perceived as being the least technologically skilled. The pupils tended to position the male teachers as experts of technology but the female teacher was positioned as little more than a passive onlooker:

> Edward: Um, well, Miss Prime doesn't really do a lot of technology. It's mainly Mr Clarke cos he's very up in that and Mr Smith, but him not so much cos he hasn't been here that long. But Miss Prime, like she sits in while we do compositions and that but no, she's not as technological. She's not as good at technology as Mr Clarke. (A level boy, Old Tech Grammar)

> Steve: I'd say that because Mr Clarke has been in the department longest but the other two are learning fast. When Mr Smith came into the school he didn't have a clue but now he can help you out with things.
> VA: And Miss Prime?
> Steve: I've never had her much for technology but she does come in during the mornings and print stuff off for orchestra. (GCSE boy, Old Tech Grammar)

Edward described the female teacher's role in the music suite as 'sitting in while we do compositions', asserting that 'she's not technological'. Steve acknowledged that she did engage with technology but this is only to 'print stuff off for orchestra'. Although he states that both Miss Prime and Mr Smith are 'learning fast' about technology, only Mr Smith is mentioned as being able to offer technological help. It was interesting to note during both observations of her teaching that Miss Prime was rather more active than Edward's comments suggest and within the course of the lesson she engaged with every pupil in the room, listening to their work on the computer and making suggestions about how it could be improved. However, unlike the types of technological interactions I witnessed between the male teachers and pupils described in the previous chapter, Miss Prime was not called upon by her A level group to engage in any technological talk as the following observation illustrates:

Miss Prime then goes over to Edward and asks him what he's working on. It's a theme and variations. She asks if she can listen to it. He says he'd rather she didn't and would rather she listen to it at the end of the lesson. She then goes over to Alistair who is working on an arrangement. She listens while he tells her about his piece. He says 'there are better ones on his computer at home' [meaning sounds] as he is not happy with the sound quality. His piece is scored for sax, trumpet, drum, piano and bass. She uses headphones to listen to his piece. She says 'good' and talks about the rhythm employed by the piano. She asks him to compare the beginning and the end of the piece: 'I feel here it's better to break them up; it's an upbeat piece therefore it keeps it moving. It feels something more interesting needs to be done with the chords'. She makes a number of musical comments but is not asked any technology related questions. (Field notes, 2nd A level observation, 24 March 2003)

Although Miss Prime teaches composition in the music technology suite where all the pupils compose, there is a perception of her as the person who teaches the technical language of composition rather than *technological* language of computers:

> Edward: I think her forte is like serialism, modern stuff. We've been doing that with her so we've been doing about minimalism, serialism, things like that; reading the rows, stuff like that. (A level boy, Old Tech Grammar)

This comment was made the day after the second A level observation cited above. Although this female teacher stated that she did not feel unconfident about working with music technology, the perception of her technological abilities are compared unfavourably to the male teachers in the department who participate in a more overt and sustained form of technological discourse, as previously described. Green (1997: 186) argues that women teachers can experience what she calls a 'refutation of their own femininity' when they display competence in an area that is not delineated as feminine, and this may help to account for why I never observed this female teacher challenge the way she was positioned by the male teachers and pupils as a technological subordinate. Male teachers and pupils engaged in technological talk asking about software or how to carry out certain technologically oriented tasks, but girls were neither encouraged to participate nor showed any signs of wishing to contribute to these technological interactions. Consequently, the combination of teachers' behaviours in the classroom and structural factors (such as not giving the female member of staff at New Tech Comprehensive suitable training) serve to construct female teachers as less technologically able than their male counterparts. Even when they are carrying out the same tasks, the perception of men's greater technological knowledge imbues them with an identity not readily available to women. As we saw in the scenario between Miss Prime and Mr Smith, this 'special knowledge' reinforces cultural assumptions about male authority and skill that reproduce gendered notions about expertise.

The pupil as expert

Studies of gender and education have argued that gender differentiation within the classroom manifests itself in numerous ways. This includes gendered teaching styles, holding differential expectations of boys and girls' educational abilities in certain subjects such as maths (Walkerdine, 1998); teachers allowing boys to dominate their attention, control classroom conversation and monopolize classroom space (Francis, 2000); displaying less tolerance towards girls' bad behaviour (Allard, 2004); and teachers not according girls' work the same value as that of boys, the latter being more likely to be seen as having more 'imagination' and 'creativity' (Clarricoates, 1978; Spender, 1982; Acker, 1994). Pupils are not passive in these gender constructions but are actively involved in these subject positionings, and it has been argued that in the music classroom teachers and pupils 'collude with each other in the perpetuation of the gender politics of music: the construction of a gendered discourse on music that aids in the regulation of gender' (Green, 1997: 186). Green's observation is certainly echoed in my findings. Throughout the classroom observations in this study, pupils were active in the construction of a technological identity that privileged boys. Even where girls displayed technological expertise, this was not necessarily acknowledged by either teachers or pupils. On the questionnaire, I specifically asked each pupil to nominate a technological expert from their class, and it was significant that all the boys nominated another boy, with the exception of Nick from Arts College. The issue of nominees was further explored during the interviews but it also sensitized me to who was being constructed as the expert and to what extent this was accepted or rejected by pupils and teachers during the lessons. An interesting example of this was observed during the three GCSE lessons at Arts College in relation to two pupils, Nick and Lisa. During their interviews, when asked to whom they turned for advice about technological matters when things went wrong they said the teacher, but they both also nominated a female pupil (Jane) who 'knew quite a lot about it [music technology]'. In addition, Nick mentioned another boy, Gary, whom he considered 'quite good at technology'. I went through my field notes again to see if Jane appeared as an expert during teacher/pupil or pupil/pupil exchanges in the previous two lessons but could find no instances of this. Consequently, during the third observation I decided to focus on who was being called upon to provide technological expertise.

As with all the previous observations at Arts College, this GCSE lesson (centred on the topic of the Viennese Waltz) was carried out in the music technology suite, taught by Miss Ellis. Referring to Strauss's 'Emperor Waltz', the class spent the first part of the double lesson discussing its musical elements before moving on to composing their own waltz in the second half of the lesson using the 'Emperor Waltz' chord sequence as the framework for their own version. When they went to their workstations, Miss Ellis told them to programme a backing rhythm in to their electronic keyboards to help them maintain the 'feel' of the waltz. Gary called out that the rhythm track went on track seventeen. The teacher said she had not realized this and pointed this out to the rest of the class. Lisa had been working quietly on her waltz for some fifteen minutes, recording the chords and playing a melody line over the top, when she encountered a problem with the computer. Despite the fact that Jane (Lisa's nominated expert) was sitting immediately to her left, she went over to Gary on the opposite side of the room to ask him to help her, which he duly did. During the remainder of the lesson two other pupils subsequently asked for his help in setting up the metronome click, and Miss Ellis also called upon Gary on two occasions when she experienced some technical problems, although on one occasion he was unable to help. He appeared happy to adopt the role of technical 'troubleshooter', making no attempt to challenge his expert positioning, and he seemed to enjoy the high-status position it placed him in. Jane, Nick and Lisa's nominated expert, did not participate in any of these technical exchanges and there were no observable moments within the lesson where Jane either requested technological help or was asked to provide it by either the teacher or pupils.

Pupils can, of course, attempt to resist or subvert these powerful discourses, but this is not always possible; individuals' own 'interpretive frameworks' (Grint and Gill, 1995) are circumscribed by the hierarchies of power constructed through social relations. In the case of Arts College, the pupils' apparent freedom to nominate a technological expert conflicted with the teacher's greater authority (and the other pupils' subsequent acceptance of this authority) to construct the expert. Gary's technological knowledge appeared to be more highly valued than that of other pupils who seemed equally competent with the technology, including Jane. The teacher's use of language (apologising to Gary on one occasion for supplying information to the rest of the class that she is aware he 'knows inside out and upside down') and her constant privileging of his technological ability over both hers and the other pupils puts Gary in the position of the expert. Consequently, the teacher's advocacy of Gary's abilities above the others reproduced a technological environment that materially and symbolically reinforced the concept of male expertise. The pupils, even when in a position to do so (such as when Lisa turned to Gary for help rather than to her neighbour Jane, her nominated expert), adhered to the teacher's greater authority and acquiesced in supporting this boy's privileged position. Oddly, this also produced an ambiguous culture in which the teacher's authoritative expert voice was undermined. Although Nick and Lisa said that they would go to the teacher first for help, I found no evidence of this during the classroom observations.

In their study, Facer et al. (2003) noted a similar construction of the male computer expert in the form of twelve-year-old David, an acknowledged ICT expert at home who soon found himself in a similar position at school with teachers and pupils calling on him for advice. He was given the responsibility of putting all the back editions of the school magazine into hypertext mark-up language

(HTML), and this expert knowledge was rewarded with special privileges, such as access to the Internet, not afforded his classmates. We can see that both Gary and David were happy to assume a technological identity which 'came from their appropriation of the symbolic power of the computer itself' allowing both boys to move effortlessly between the world of childhood and adults (Facer et al., 2003: 116) by receiving adult affirmation of their technological abilities. Both boys were given greater levels of responsibility, and teachers would defer to their greater technical skills and knowledge.

It is not therefore simply a case of examining the role education plays in reproducing dominant codes and identities, but also of acknowledging that individuals are involved in the active construction of their own complex identity positions (Dillabough, 2001), suggesting that the construction of technological cultures involve strategies and counter-strategies of power, *active* positionings which may allow new meanings and discourses to emerge. However, individuals' interpretive frameworks are embedded within existing social spaces that are already delineated along gender lines and which imbue their experiences with meaning. Consequently, gender behaviour and relations are a process of accommodation and mutual acceptance (Reay, 2001), which was certainly in evidence at Arts College. Even where individuals seem able to construct their own meanings around technological expertise, these can be easily countered when pupils are faced with the teacher's authoritative construction of a culture that privileges boys' skills and expertise.

This does not mean that the dominant discourse of a technological masculinity cannot be subverted, but it can be difficult for those who are positioned outside of that discourse. However, I did observe one instance of girls attempting to construct their own expert that ran counter to the dominant discourse within the classroom. During my first GCSE observation at Old Tech Grammar I had noticed a group of three girls talking together during a composition lesson in the music technology suite. Although each had been working independently on her own composition at an individual workstation, one of the girls, Vanessa, had gone over to help Gemma, who was experiencing some difficulties notating her blues piece. After about ten minutes Vanessa went back to her computer but she did not seem to be working. I went over to her and found out that she had completed her piece, which she invited me to listen to through her headphones. We then chatted informally about how she had composed the piece. She also stated she was a very confident technology user, having the relevant software at home, but commented that she did not like composing and preferred playing (she had taken grade 8 Associated Board exams in two instruments). Having collated the information from the questionnaires, I was aware that she was only one of two girls across all four schools (together with Jane as discussed above) nominated as technological expert. Unlike the boys' reasons for nominating their experts, the girls who nominated Vanessa emphasized different qualities that did not directly relate to technology, such as her ability to explain things clearly, and her sensitivity and patience. The girls associated certain qualities with their technological expert that stood outside of the prevailing discourse of masculine expertise at this school:

> VA: Right. So you've nominated Vanessa as your expert. Is she the person you go to most of all for help?
> Gemma: Yeah, because she'll, she's really patient with us. She'll explain things and also she's really helpful. She'll listen to what you've done, say 'that sounds good but perhaps you could put it in a different key to make it sound better' and things like that.

These sentiments were echoed by Joanne, who had also nominated Vanessa:

> VA: When you come across various problems who do you normally ask for help when you're here [in the music technology suite]?
> Joanne: When I'm here there's a girl in my class, Vanessa.
> VA: Yeah, you put her as your technological expert. The one who's really good…
> Joanne: She's been really nice, yeah. And sometimes, it's like the teachers are dotted about and you can't find them straight away and she's always there to help. Um, if I need a second opinion or something then I know she's going to be truthful and help me out. If it's rubbish she'll tell me. (GCSE girl, Old Tech Grammar)

Looking at these comments, even though I framed the question within the context of nominating a *technological* expert, the girls' reasons for nominating Vanessa do not specifically refer to aspects of technology but focus on her musical and personal qualities such as her ability to listen and give good critical advice. She is described as 'nice', 'patient' and 'helpful', qualities that her female classmates value when asking for advice and help.

Gemma had also nominated Robert as an expert, but her reasons were completely different from those she gave regarding Vanessa. Robert's ability to work 'for hours … four days solidly' on his piece was given as a reason to nominate him as an expert, even though the questionnaire had specifically asked pupils to nominate a classmate based on his or her technological expertise. This particular mode of working has been observed in male computer hackers, who take great pride in being able to work for extremely long hours without stopping. MIT hackers call this 'sport death', where the mind and body are pushed beyond their limits by denying themselves food or sleep (Turkle, 1988). I would suggest that Gemma's perception of Robert's expertise was, in part, connected to this rather macho image of the male computer expert, and it was interesting to note how little it resembled the feminine form of technological expertise attributed to Vanessa. The skill and status associated with boys' engagement with technology reinforce the symbolic association of masculinity with technology and must be maintained at all times, often at the expense of female pupils and teachers whose knowledge is not accorded the same value. Men's engagement with technology must continue the illusion that their expertise is highly valuable, and the skills needed to engage with technology must be redefined to maintain gender relations that denigrate women's knowledge and skill.

Gendering music software

So far, this chapter has been concerned with the ways in which expertise is constructed as an essential part of masculine identity, through a demonstration of how gendered discourses about technical skills are reproduced in the music classroom in the construction of the technological expert. As such, the technological artefact can be seen as part of a social system, intrinsic to the ways in which certain types of social relations are produced and maintained. The remainder of this chapter will develop this theme showing how the notion of masculine skill and expertise is also integral to the way in which discourses around music software produce gendered connotations whereby software perceived as requiring greater technological skill carries more status than that which is regarded as easy to use. Instead of simply saying technological artefacts are either 'tool-like, devoid of politics' or that they are 'instruments of oppression' (Faulkner, 2001), we can look at the ways that gender relations are contained and constructed *by* technological artefacts that give a material form to the mutual shaping of gender and technology.

Across the four schools a variety of music software was in use, ranging from score-writing notational packages such as Sibelius to MIDI sequencing software such as Cubase, and quite basic recording software such as Cakewalk, but significant gendered differences emerged regarding the use of the software and perceptions of the level of expertise required to use it. It has been argued that the design and complexity of types of music software come to reflect an 'ideal' user whereby the design and utilitarian intention of the artefact may encourage some uses while prohibiting others, shaping the meaning of that artefact. As Yates and Littleton (2001: 111) argue, both the content and the context of software can offer a preferred reading which allows the take-up of some subject positions while inhibiting others. Women often experience problems when negotiating male-gendered, preferred readings within very violent or sexist computer games that may not appeal to girls (Kiesler et al., 1985; Kirkup et al., 1992; Sofia, 1998) but are written in a way that assumes a particular (male) audience (Cooper, 2006).

Winner (1999) argues that we must take technical artefacts seriously and not reduce everything simply to the interplay of social forces. He is interested in examining the characteristics of technological objects and the *meanings* of these characteristics and, from this perspective, he argues that technologies can be said to contain political properties that come to represent forms of power and authority. Bromley (1997) asserts that technologies are not infinitely malleable and cannot be put to absolutely any end at will, and thus to over-emphasize the context of use leads to the problem of assuming that the impact of a technology is wholly determined by the intent of its users. Like Winner, he believes that there is a dialectical relationship between what he calls the 'bias' contained within the technology and the context of use, which is transmitted through the social nature of its design and development. We can see how this may manifest itself as a 'gender script' defined as 'assumptions about a supposed user that becomes an integral part of an entire process of technological development' (Heemskerk et al., 2009: 254), which result in the design of technological objects that inscribe a vision of the world in the content of the object (Tjora, 2009). Mindful that this may appear over-determining, writers are at pains to point out that this is not to deny individual agency as scripts can be modified and rejected. Heemskerk et al. (2009) argued that the extent to which the script is adhered to will depend on the context of its use and decisions made by the users. However, as I noted earlier, in the classroom, the gendered cultural setting in which the technological object is situated may make it difficult for pupils to resist or subvert these gendered scripts. If we acknowledge this possibility, we would have to consider how decisions about technological design may have been developed with a particular agenda in mind that may best serve the interests of certain social groups to the detriment of others. In this sense, the political properties Winner (1999) speaks of also have an ideological function. The artefact's design may have been carried out by groups who have a particular interest, or make presuppositions related to their own needs, in maintaining certain social relations which may prove difficult to reconfigure within the possibilities available from the artefact by other less powerful groups.

Feminizing technology

Green (1997: 101) observes that using the label feminine not only expresses ideas about the characteristics of femininity (and masculinity) but is also a value judgement. As such, feminine technologies, like feminine music (when applied to women), are denigrated and positioned as lesser and inferior to those that are considered masculine. Consequently, feminine technologies are considered easier to use and to require less skill to operate them, and gendered ideologies are embedded in a range of technologies largely designed by men but intended for use by women. Examining the development of the domestic washing machine, Alemany Gomez (1994) noted that one particular design team sought the views of the engineers' wives. She argues that a particular ideology is being invoked here that strengthens gendered expectations about women's ability to manipulate technology. Envisioning the female user, the male engineer imagines the 'errors' that might be made during the washing machine's use, resulting in scenarios depicting women's 'clumsiness' and 'technical ignorance' requiring the implementation of devices which would prevent the machine from malfunctioning however inept its user: as the technicians put it, in case 'the women were absent mindedly to open the door during the washing cycle' or 'a child were to open the machine', the female user being conflated with the naughty child in the eyes of the engineers. Similarly, Berg's (1994) research into the 'Honeywell smart house' replete with hi-tech gadgets also points to an imagined user. Illustrating the workings of an automatic light switch, the designer asserts this would be a useful gadget because the 'housewife' entering a room with her arms full of wet clothes would not have to put them down to switch on the light. These examples demonstrate the gender scripts embedded in the innovation process, sociotechnical constructs reflecting an imagined gendered user. While Berg believes that technology can be open to flexible interpretation she finds little evidence of this within the smart house.

Feminizing music technology

It has been suggested that some types of computer interfaces are better suited to female users. For example, the Apple Mac interface, with its simulated desktop, introduced a way of thinking that put a premium on surface manipulation through pointing and clicking on an icon, the user apparently ignorant of (and not interested in) its underlying mechanisms (Turkle, 1995). Hapnes and Sorensen (1995) make a similar point, arguing that Apple Mac computers are symbolically associated with women because they are well structured and rule-based, which makes them simpler to use. In contrast, men are more likely to express dislike for software that represents uniform and rule-regulated systems as it inhibits their freedom and ability to operate within a more complex computer environment. Men like to see themselves as being able to experiment with computer programs on a more free and intuitive basis rather than being 'forced' to interact with them in what they would perceive as a rather didactic way of working.

This suggests that meanings attributed to music composition software in the classroom require a more critical examination in light of the arguments above to interrogate how it is implicated in the construction of gendered identities. It appears that within the music classroom the appropriation of certain types of software as being compatible with high levels of skill is an important aspect of boys' masculine identity. When women take on the work that men do, that work is often viewed as having become de-skilled and degraded. Females, even when engaged with technology, are positioned in such a way that the similar status accorded to males is not conferred. In this way, the design and complexity (or simplicity) of music software enters into the construction of gendered identities.

The different meanings pupils construct around the software and the software's capabilities carry different values. Caputo argues that, for female pupils, 'there are conceptual and value-laden agendas in the software and presentation of music technology that reflect mainstream ways of knowing' (1994: 89). It appears that score-writing notational packages (where the screen interface resembles a piece of manuscript paper) such as Music Time Deluxe and Sibelius are perceived in this way because they are considered to involve very little technological skill. The music can be inputted either via a MIDI keyboard or via the mouse, using the keypad with the mouse to specify rhythm and pitch:

> Peter: I just find Sibelius really simple. It's just easy to put a note down, you know, conventional notation. (A level boy, Crossways Independent)

Carolyn: Um, well it depends what you mean by music technology because I don't really think Sibelius is what I really think of as technology because my brother is doing music technology and it's all keyboards, mixing desks and things like that. (A level girl, Crossways Independent)

Craig: They sometimes use Music Time Deluxe here [at school] but it's a bit rubbish really, so generally, if I was doing sequencing stuff, I'd do that at home using Cubase or Logic.[1] (A level boy, Old Tech Grammar)

Gemma: I can only use Music Time Deluxe and I think a couple of my friends are like that. He [The teacher] talks about others like Cubase and stuff but we're just not sure how to use them. I mean, some of the boys, like Robert, he's really, really good with the computer and you listen to some of his stuff and it's really fantastic …
VA: Do you see yourself getting that into computers?
Gemma: Compared to that [Cubase], I mean Music Time Deluxe isn't that, it's pretty basic really. It's just mainly putting things on. You can't really experiment with it. It's just, you just put something on and it plays it back and prints it out. That's all it does. I haven't been taught how to use any of the other pieces of software so I'm limited to that really. (GCSE girl, Old Tech Grammar)

From the comments above, both boys and girls make a distinction between the apparently simple notation packages, such as Music Time Deluxe and Sibelius, and sequencing software, leading Carolyn to observe that she does not really think of the Sibelius software as technology compared to the 'real' and more complex music technologies used by her brother. Gemma also negatively evaluates Music Time Deluxe when compared to Robert's use of the sequencing package Cubase, which enables him to 'experiment', whereas her perception of Music Time Deluxe appears to be as little more than a storage device: you input the notes, they are played back to you, and then you print out the music. As Gemma notes, 'that's all it does'. In fact, Music Time Deluxe does have a basic editing facility but it is not a dedicated package in the same way as Cubase or Logic, leading Craig to assert that Music Time Deluxe was 'rubbish'. However, none of the girls mentioned using the sequencing capabilities of Music Time Deluxe, usually stating that they worked with the score editor which, like Sibelius, was notation centred.

---

[1]   Logic Studio is designed for use with Apple Macs, and is often used by professional musicians. It can be used for multi-track recording and MIDI sequencing, and offers a wide range of plugs-in. At the time of gathering the data for this book, Logic was never mentioned as a software teachers used in the classroom – Cubase VST was the most commonly used of the MIDI sequencing packages. It should be noted that, throughout the book, I have used definitions for music software that were correct in 2005 as this was the software referred to at the time. However, I recognize that software names and functions may well have been changed or updated in the intervening years.

Even when boys do use Sibelius, there is a tendency to emphasize their musical skills to counteract what they perceive as the simpler aspects of the software:

> Craig: Yeah. I don't sort of click it in, like one note at a time, I actually play it in, play the chords, play the whole thing. (A level boy, New Tech Comprehensive)

> Edward: Well, Sibelius I've had for quite a while. I've had it since it first came out, my parents bought it for me, so I've been using that for a while now and I can do a lot on that ... On things like Sibelius, if you're a competent pianist like me, you can just press the record button and you can just play it in and it'll all come up very quickly. (A level boy, Old Tech Grammar)

> Peter: Well, Sibelius is fine for what I need it for. But what really matters are the chords. If you're composing a piece you need chords, so I'd probably concentrate on playing in the chords and then sort of do, then write a melody over that. (A level boy, Crossways Independent)

This compares sharply to Joanne's comments about using Sibelius and her negative appraisal of her skills:

> Joanne: Sometimes I play it in if it's quite simple but if there's like complicated bits then I'll usually click it in or I can play a bar and if it's repeated I'll just copy and paste it all the way through. I know I'm not gonna get the rhythm right so I'll just click it in cos it saves a lot of time. (GCSE girl, Old Tech Grammar)

Comber et al. (1993: 130) make a similar observation whereby the masculine perception of the simplicity of music technology led one boy to comment that 'You don't have to be a musician to make music now. Using computers, anyone off the street can just make a number one hit. I like acoustic instruments, that's what music's about really, not all computerized sounds.' The more software resembles traditional notation, the less it is perceived as requiring any particular skill and was derided as being 'easy' or 'rubbish' compared to 'real' sequencing packages. There is little cachet attached to using what are perceived as 'simple' forms of technology, and these notational packages may have acquired feminine connotations because of their association with classical music genres and traditional instruments. This chimes with Hugill's (2008) assertion that a composer using a notation package to write a string quartet cannot claim to be a 'digital musician'. Using technology as a tool is not enough but must include a level of creativity that goes beyond what the composer is currently able to achieve non-digitally in order to merit this description. Therefore, the pupils' assertion that notational software does not require 'real' musical or technical skill reinforces the distinction between those who use sequencing software (and constitute the true 'digital musician') and those who do not, and this distinction is highly gendered. Ann Southam, a Canadian composer (McCartney, 1995) describes her first experiences using music 'electronics' in the University of Toronto studio in the 1960s working with oscillators, filters and loop machines, and found this a very positive experience. However, she makes the comment that 'Fortunately, I think the equipment was so unsophisticated that it couldn't possibly be thought of as mathematical' (and therefore not associated with the complex and the masculine). She continued working with new electronic instruments into the late 1980s but gradually stopped working in this way, explaining that she lost affinity with the instruments because they removed the 'hands-on approach' she had developed working by hand and ear: 'Working by numbers on a computer screen – I just couldn't relate to it … I just couldn't relate to looking at the sound.'[2] This reflects Wajcman's assertion that:

> Men's relationship to technology is defined differently to women's. Cultural notions of masculinity stress competence in the use and repair of machines. Machines are extensions of male power and signal men's control of the environment. Women can be users of machines, particularly those to do with housework, but this is not seen as a competence with technology. Women's use of machines, unlike men's, is not seen as a mark of their skill. Women's identity is not enhanced by their use of machines. (Wajcman, 1991: 89)

Consequently, the mere engagement with machines is not, in itself, enough to secure an acceptable technological identity. It is the nature of that engagement and, as I have suggested, using 'gender appropriate' software is one way that boys and girls construct acceptable identities. Software perceived as requiring less technological skill to manipulate it is aligned with femininity and may lead boys to reject it. Using notational software appears to offer boys very little in the construction of an affirmatory masculinity, which, unlike femininity, must be associated with technology that is perceptibly more challenging, complex, skilled and status-conferring.

Masculinizing music technology

Consequently, in light of the above, an important aspect of the construction of masculinity is through perceived ability to manipulate sequencing software that requires higher levels of technological skill:

> VA: Tell me why you think Alan is good at using technology.
> Edward: Well, he's a good musician and he does a lot at home as well I think. I don't really know him too well but he always seems to know what he's doing in the studio and that. I think it's quite a big hobby for him. He does a lot of composing in his spare time on kind of Cubase and programmes like that so he's got like a better background and knowledge. He just seems very competent

---

[2]   No page numbers are given for this journal article.

when he's using the computers and recording equipment. (A level boy, Old Tech Grammar)

VA: Why do you think Alan [is good at using technology]?
Craig: I dunno. He just seems to know how everything works, he's just picked it up. Don't know why. Maybe he's read it or I dunno.
VA: If you get stuck do you actually ask him for help?
Craig: If he's around yeah. If he's not around I try and figure it out for myself but if he's there I'll ask him. He usually knows.
VA: So why do you think he's better than you?
Craig: Dunno really. I think one of the reasons is his multi-track is very, very good, so he obviously knows quite a bit about the recording side, like setting up and stuff. (A level boy, Old Tech Grammar)

Game and Pringle (1984) suggest that it is necessary for men to maintain the 'mystification of machines' in order to preserve not only male jobs and wage rates but the symbolic association of men's work with skill. If women worked on the machines, it would show how stationary and repetitive these tasks were, but by insisting that only men work with them this further loss of control of the work process could be disguised. Thus, men are able to represent the power of the machine as theirs and experience themselves as having a monopoly on 'technical expertise', as status and skill are intrinsic to definitions of men's work. As Bayton suggests, in jobs perceived as 'endowing masculine status, if women start doing them, such status conferral will be undermined' (1998: 8). Consequently, as both boys and girls now use technology in the music classroom it may be that boys need to experience themselves as expert sequencers to enable them to (re)claim the symbolic association of technology with masculinity.

The separation of acceptable masculine and feminine technologies is bound up with the meanings that are attributed to that technology in terms of whether or not engaging with it affirms our notion of how technological skill and expertise are implicated in the construction of a gendered identity. It has been noted that younger girls are often more enthusiastic about using music technology than adolescent girls and it has been suggested this may be because the technology involved concentrates on electronic keyboards, which are perceived as a *musical instrument* and not a technology (Colley et al., 1997). Consequently, if adolescent girls are expected to use more complex sequencing packages, defined as a masculine technology, this may prove highly contradictory for their sense of feminine identity, particularly as adolescents appear to conform more overtly to cultural assumptions about what is appropriately masculine or feminine than do their younger counterparts.

At Old Tech Grammar and New Tech Comprehensive boys were significantly more likely to talk about software packages such as Cool Edit Pro, Logic,

Cubase and Reason.[3] Although all of the boys interviewed at Old Tech Grammar had achieved Grade 6 or above in Associated Board examinations on at least one instrument, they presented themselves as particular types of musicians and composers who could comfortably straddle the world of digitally mediated composition and popular music, and many were involved in bands out of school. The A level boys who inhabited the music studio at Old Tech Grammar and the boys from New Tech Comprehensive were keen to portray a particular type of masculine identity that combined being technologically knowledgeable, musically adventurous and well able to work with 'electronic music':

> Craig: It's because I record guitars and stuff. Cos what I do on computer is mainly stuff for my brother's band, then I use Reason as a drum machine and record that as a Wav file and then record guitars and bass. Obviously, like electronic stuff like Reason, the drum beats are all tab operated so if you have 16 tabs and you can click on 1, 5, 9 and 13 then it just does that [claps], the first beat of every note, it's just divided into semiquavers so that's quite good with electronic stuff. (A level boy, Old Tech Grammar)

> Joe: I always use the keyboard, and for most of my songs. I usually have an alto sax playing the sort of leads. That's mainly what I use but I don't usually play the sax to write. I put it on there, I've got the programme Reason and that's um sort of pop dance music based and I made about ten songs on there since I got it cos I enjoy using that program a lot. I've made ten fairly different songs on it and it's really good.
> VA: What do you like about it [Reason]?
> Joe: Probably because it's different from all the others. It's a hardware simulation instead of just a program cos it's got the um, it's a sequencer and it's also got the actual synthesizers and samplers. You can actually see them and if you sort of, if you press the tab, you can see behind the back and see all the wires. It's really good. (A level boy, New Tech Comprehensive)

These comments and Joe's enthusiasm for being able to (virtually) 'see all the wires' reinforce the envisaging of an ideal *male* user, as sound engineering remains a very male-dominated field where entrenched notions of masculinity prevail (Sandstrom, 2000; Smaill, 2005). Therefore, the way this software is designed may pander to the perceived interests of a particular type of user who is interested in manipulating controls that allow the user to generate very loud sounds and 'boxy tones' to produce the type of aggressive, nasal drum loops often used to create dance music forms. These design features could therefore be seen

---

[3]   Cool Edit Pro software is used for digital audio recording with built-in editing and mixing facilities but is not a sequencer. Reason acts as a virtual music studio that replicates a hardware rack setup of a traditional sound engineer. It has a mixing desk, effects units, loop players and drum machines.

to reproduce the symbolic gendering of the archetypal male user with its emphasis on loudness and aggression:

> In general, when boys in schools perform 'popular music' or 'fast music', play drums and electric instruments, or manipulate technology, they are furthering a symbolic representation of their masculinity [...] Contrastingly, when girls sing, and when they play 'slow' music, or 'classical' music on orchestral instruments, they are furthering a powerful symbolization of their femininity. (Green, 1997: 185)

As Frith and McRobbie (1978/9) note, male forms of rock music are often loud, aggressive and rhythmically insistent, constructing a desirable identity of heterosexual masculinity. The design features of Reason software reinforce these assumptions about the potential user and this user is normatively male.

Interestingly, this male identification with rock music can also enable those boys who are less interested or less confident in using music software to engage with simpler technologies without challenging their masculinity. Patrick from New Tech Comprehensive stated that 'I do use Cubase for composing although I find it difficult' then contradicted himself by asserting that 'it's simple to use; you can put stuff straight into the computer'. However, I never observed him using the computer during composition lessons and this was reinforced by his class teacher's comments that Patrick rarely used sequencing software and was more likely to be found playing on his electric guitar in a practice room. This was supported by Patrick's description of his approach to composition, which was very low tech compared to other boys in his class:

> VA: Can you describe a piece of music you've written recently in as much detail as possible?
> Patrick: Well, the last composition I done was a film piece. I started it off with the guitar with just a basic tune and I just extended on that. I had an image of, well the sound of my piece was to fit a kind of desert scene, on a motorbike going along. There's a woman who's trying to get home and the husband's been, like, killed, but she don't know about it. And I put, like, xylophones in it and some drums.
> VA: Did you do that on Cubase?
> Patrick: No. I done it on this recording thing and I was still playing my guitar.
> VA: So when did the computer come into the process?
> Patrick: I didn't use it in my last piece actually. I prefer just to use the recording stuff.
> VA: Just explain that to me. This recording stuff you talk about...?
> Patrick: The minidisk recording thing. You can get eight different sounds on it. I just played lots of different tracks. (GCSE boy, New Tech Comprehensive)

Interestingly, Patrick's lack of engagement with computer technology and his apparent inability to demonstrate technological expertise did not appear to compromise his sense of identity. At his school very few of the male GCSE pupils took formal instrumental lessons or played orchestral instruments to a high standard, the majority being drummers and guitarists (over 70 per cent stated they played in a band of some kind outside of school). Presenting themselves as rock musicians was an acceptable and desirable masculine identity amongst these pupils. In contrast, women are not expected to engage with the actual technologies of rock, such as electric guitars, drums and amplifiers (Cohen, 1991; Bayton, 1997), because

> rock is associated with technology, which is itself symbolically interwoven with masculinity. Boys get given technological toys: girls do not. Boys' informal learning, in the home and amongst their peers, breeds a familiarity with, and confidence in, all things mechanical and scientific. (Bayton, 1998: 41)

Therefore, even though Patrick's compositional approach generally eschewed affirmatory 'masculine' software such as Cubase, his guitar-focused approach to composing, and his construction of himself as a rock musician, enabled him to successfully construct an alternative but equally acceptable affirmatory technological identity.

Conclusion

This chapter has attempted to show the cultural and material factors that contribute to on-going notions of expertise and masculinity, and who is able to participate in the production of discourses of expertise. By rendering the girls largely silent in this construction, the values generated by males can lead to an environment that affords little merit to the values that girls attributed to 'expertise'. The cultural landscape and the discursive practices of the teachers and pupils work to produce this 'silencing' and is a situation found in a number of sites in which women's knowledge is undervalued. However, I noted that, despite having technological knowledge and skill, the girls and female teachers, when in the classroom, have less power to actively position themselves as skilled users, and find themselves positioned by the male 'experts' as less competent and skilled users within a technologically oriented music environment. Consequently, within these classroom cultures, where technical skill in manipulating computers is highly valued, boys who are good at technology can position themselves as successful males. I argued that this was implicit in the values attached to the music software both in its design and in pupils' perceptions of its simplicity or complexity, these perceptions feeding into notions of what constitutes 'feminine' and 'masculine' technology.

Design choices can be made with gendered assumptions about the users in mind, and show how the gendering of artefacts can also be *by association,* whereby the symbolism attached to technology influences our perception and understanding of technology. Therefore, it becomes apparent that preferences and uses of music software are an important way of expressing identity. Such arguments go some way to providing a more sophisticated analysis that does not see all technology as inherently masculine but acknowledges both the material and symbolic associations which contribute to the gendering of the artefact and thus removes the possibility of labelling all technologies as alien to women. This reinforces the position adopted throughout this book that urges teachers working with music technology to take a more socially embedded view of technology which explores how different social groups construct their own meanings around technologies and how the innate 'politics' embedded within the design of the technological artefact produces certain types of social relations.

Chapter 5
Gendering the Musical Idea

In Chapters 3 and 4 I identified how material and cultural processes and practices – in the form of gendered talk, interaction and expectations about technological engagement and the construction of space – powerfully contribute to gendered discourses that young composers in school must learn to negotiate in their gendered constructions of themselves and others as technological/non-technological, expert/ non-expert, skilled/unskilled. Having explored the sociocultural context in which music composition is carried out, this chapter attempts to illuminate the extent to which these gendered processes and practices are played out with regard to the origins of the *musical idea* and issues of deviance and conformity, a recurring issue in pupils' accounts of their compositions.

Paynter (2000: 9) is critical of the loose way in which the term 'musical idea' is often employed. He makes a distinction between the composer's *intention* (as in the stimulus for the musical work, which can be anything from a musical structure to a text or picture) and the *musical idea* (which would be the actual musical materials). He states that the composer's intention is part of the 'context'; this context is the pre-musical form through which the composer begins to think about the piece, and can be based on a musical or non-musical element. It can take the form of a literary idea, a combination of sounds, or a musical form such as a fugue or sonata; it is not what the music is actually 'about', but 'although it might be described as "an idea for music" it is not the same as a musical idea!' (Paynter, 2000: 9). However, in light of my respondents' comments about the origins of the 'musical idea', the careful distinction Paynter makes between the intention and the musical idea is somewhat blurred. My findings shows that pupils' musical ideas often emanate from the teacher's intention, so this distinction is less tenable than perhaps it might otherwise be in a situation where the composer herself has control over this aspect of the compositional process. In light of this blurring my adoption of 'musical idea' aims to encapsulate both stimulus and musical materials and will help to illuminate how compositional and gendered identities are implicated in this crucial stage of the process.

The musical idea

Although it is common practice to provide a musical idea as a stimulus for composition there is some anxiety about this practice amongst music educators. Plummeridge (1981) has long questioned the educational value of giving ideas to children of other composers' work on which they should base their process, although it remains an integral part of teaching composition and 'learning by copying has a noble precedent' (Paterson and Odam, cited in Bunting, 2002: 171). Savage[1] states that classroom composition is a subculture conceptualized and practised in an 'inauthentic' way as distinct from what he would argue are the 'authentic' practices of DJs, classical composers and popular musicians. He argues that even where pupils are familiar with certain styles, such as popular song genre, this can lead to an over prescription of content and formalization of ideas. Glover (2000) also highlights this by arguing that, despite teachers' beliefs that children come into school trying to compose without musical models, children do have a wide range of experiences of musical models acquired through enculturation and it is the teacher's task to uncover what pupils bring with them into the classroom. Enculturation is not about musical training and skill but about children's musical development in relation to their sense of the music around them and how they wish their own compositions to relate to this (Sloboda, cited in Glover, 2000). This leads Glover to assert that 'it is when they [*the children*] come up with their own ideas for what the music will be that it becomes most meaningful to them' (2000: 27). This is supported by Hickey's (1997) belief that fewer rules lead to a product that is more artistically creative. It may be open to debate as to what constitutes artistic creativity; however, her assertion that 'the more constraints or boundaries delineated in a given problem, the less problem finding and room for divergent thinking is left up to the individual' (1997: 64) is a more straightforward and perhaps less contentious reason for encouraging individuals to work from their own stimulus.

The musical idea, self-expression and ownership

One of the teachers from New Tech Comprehensive stated that 'I certainly feel very frustrated in front of a blank screen or a new Cubase sequencing file and don't know where to start, and I think that is difficult for all composers', an experience well documented in accounts of professional composers' working practices:[2]

> I can drag myself out of bed to do some work every day whether I am inspired or not. I can't trust my inspiration that much. I've really only composed a few, what I consider, truly inspired pieces. If I relied on inspiration rather than processes I would never get anything done. (American composer Mary Lee Roberts in Hinkle-Turner et al., 1999: 6)

---

[1]   No date is available for this on-line report, which appears on the website for PALATINE (the UK Higher Education subject centre for dance, drama and music), www.lancaster.ac.uk/palantine/jons-article.htm.

[2]   It is interesting to note that Griffith's (1985) book, based on the compositional practices of twenty British composers born after 1932, only interviews male composers, despite his stated aim that the book encapsulates a 'wide variety of styles and personalities' (1985: 9).

Thus, starting a new piece from scratch is a challenge all composers must face, but invention and generation of musical materials are obviously fundamental starting points for any composer, and yet teachers, guided by music curriculum requirements, do not hesitate to provide an initial stimulus for a compositional activity (such as a chord sequence, or type of scale) on which the pupils are expected to base their composition. While this allows the teacher to implement the necessary prescriptions of the syllabus, this may also reflect an ideology about the value of certain kinds of music, musical knowledge and medium of composition (Green, 2003) and may not reflect the values and meanings that the pupils themselves construct about their music:

> Patrick: I listen to a lot of rock music.
> VA: And do you think this influences your compositions?
> Patrick: Yeah.
> VA: To what extent?
> Patrick: I take quite a lot of ideas from it.
> VA: Right, what kind of ideas? Rhythmic or chords?
> Patrick: Tunes and stuff. I don't copy them [emphatically]. I just take the idea and play around with it.
> [...]
> VA: What do you like and dislike about composing generally?
> Patrick: I don't like doing it when you have to do it like the teacher says.
> VA: Would you rather do your own stuff?
> Patrick: Yeah. Like the set compositions, the teacher decides.
> VA: What if you were providing your own stimulus?
> Patrick: I'd be happier with that, cos I'd do what I wanna do. It would sound better. Otherwise I'm doing what he wants to make it sound right. (GCSE boy, New Tech Comprehensive)

Examining the relationship between the genesis of the musical idea with issues of self-expression and ownership is important in understanding how this contributes to a young composer's sense of musical and gendered identity. Giving pupils 'freedom of choice' can increase both enjoyment and levels of motivation in the music classroom setting; having autonomy over curriculum content better reflects pupils' interests and musical identities (Green, 2008).

Interestingly, working with musical ideas provided by teachers elicited similarly negative responses from both boys and girls. Although some pupils stated they liked the boundaries provided by a given musical idea, the majority saw such stimuli as removing a sense ownership or pride in their work, as Carolyn passionately stated:

> Carolyn: I find if you're given an idea and told to stick with that idea, then I'm like 'But I didn't want to go in that way', so, you're always proud of yourself when you come away with a composition that sounds sort of good, but then you

do sort of, there's not much emotional attachment to the piece. I suppose that's a bit of shame because that's what music's about for me. (A level girl, Crossways Independent)

This sense of 'emotional attachment', pride and self-expression were very strong themes in the comments about their work of girls from all four schools:

VA: The stuff that you compose. What do you think its purpose is, apart from fulfilling coursework obligations?

Joanne: Well, I suppose it has got some kind of meaning in it. The things you do from scratch or something is more meaningful because it's something you've started from the beginning but if you've got, you're like told to do something along these lines, it's not as meaningful because you've been told like half of what you're supposed to do. (GCSE girl, Old Tech Grammar)

VA: Tell me what you like about composing.

Lisa: Well, you can use it to express yourself. (GCSE girl, Arts College)

Alice: It's quite expressive in the way that you can do it, especially as I write sad sounding pieces, but it's kind of expressive and really personal because it's all like your idea and you can feel quite proud of it that you made it up. (GCSE girl, New Tech Comprehensive)

Laura: I don't try to be expressive but when people listen to it they're like 'Ah, that's really expressive'. They seem to be able to tell things. (A level girl, New Tech Comprehensive)

The composer Hinkle-Turner (in Hinkle-Turner et al., 1999: 3) asserts that the combination of 'heart and head' is essential when composing, a combination she stated was missing from her own work while carrying out postgraduate study as she 'tried very hard to write music that pleased [her] professors'. However, this self-expressive element could actually be problematic for some of the girls, particularly when their compositions were based on their own musical ideas, which 'all come from you'. When their work is criticized this can feel like a very personal attack and can have a negative impact on their evaluation of their own compositional abilities:

VA: Do you like composing?

Karen: Yeah. Well, it's a chance to be creative. It can be as personal as you want it to be. I think it's the best part of doing music really.

VA: And do you feel confident with your compositions?

Karen: I think I can improve quite a lot. There's definitely room for improvement.

VA: Do you tend to change or stick to your original ideas when people criticize you?

Karen: Depends on how certain I was about it in the first place. If I was a bit sort of, wasn't quite sure and then they said it was bad then yes, I'd change it. Sometimes my friend Kezia, we tend to play things to each other but we don't really say anything horrible. (GCSE girl, Crossways Independent)

VA: What else do you like about thinking up your own ideas?
Kezia: There's no boundaries. I just like writing music [...] It's just interesting. We can do what we want. Like written work you have to do what the teacher tells you. Composing, we can get our own ideas. It makes you think more.
VA: Do you see composing as anything to do with self-expression?
Kezia: It's a bit personal because it all comes from you. A teacher can't, like if you were writing an essay they tell you what to go on. Composing is all down to you.
VA: How do you feel when people criticize your music?
Kezia: Criticism is always, it helps. It does feel a bit weird but I learn from it. (GCSE girl, Crossways Independent)

VA: Would you say you're confident about your compositions?
Joanne: I think I'm confident about them [hesitates] but I'm, I don't know. I just worry about what other people think about it.
VA: In what way?
Joanne: Well, if you started something from scratch and you think it's good and someone tells you it's not then it's sort of, don't know, sort of quite nasty. Because if you're doing like a bit of coursework you have guidelines like in other subjects, but if you do this and start it from scratch, so it's all like what you thought.
VA: Why do you think it's more difficult to deal with if somebody criticizes your work then?
Joanne: It feels like a personal thing when people criticize your music, when they're criticizing about something you've done. I might ask somebody else what they think as well and then see if I can improve it from there. Cos if somebody else thinks it's bad, the whole thing is bad. (GCSE girl, Old Tech Grammar)

On the whole, boys were less inclined to talk of their personal feelings in relation to their compositions, and expressed none of the concerns articulated by the girls cited above:

VA: Do you feel your compositions say anything about you? A form of self-expression perhaps?
Ian: No.
VA: Absolutely no?
Ian: No! [Laughs] (GCSE boy, Crossways Independent)

> VA: Do you feel your music expresses anything about you?
> Craig: No.
> VA: Does it have any meaning for you?
> Craig: I dunno about meaningful. It's just whether you like it or not. (A level
> boy, Old Tech Grammar)

Even if boys do feel that their music has a self-expressive quality, they appear to find it difficult to articulate this, some boys making knowingly trite remarks during their interviews. Luke, from Crossways Independent, was considered by his teacher and peers to be a highly competent classical guitarist and composer, and his music was often performed both in and out of school. During his interview, he would occasionally become very animated when talking about his compositional ideas and appeared to spend a lot of his spare time outside of school composing, but he seemed unable to commit himself to openly stating that composing was meaningful for him:

> VA: Tell me what composing means to you.
> Luke: I think it, um, it expr... well, um, it generally functions, I don't know if
> I'm ever, um. When I get home from school I'll play [my guitar] for a couple
> of hours, well not a couple of hours, say for about an hour [...] and, I dunno
> composing it um, I think you um, it's important to my life. I dunno I think it's
> quite nice to see how it affects people, if you play something and it sounds
> incredible or whatever it changes them, well not changed them but made them,
> well had some impact on them then that makes me, well, kind of chuffed. I
> mean, um, for me I think, um, it kind of, its purpose is, um, to get a decent grade
> at GCSE [laughing]! (GCSE boy, Crossways Independent)

Having initially responded quite openly about the role of music in his life and clearly appearing pleased that his music had an 'impact' on his listeners, it was evident that Luke felt a little uncomfortable talking in this way and abruptly cut short further exploration of this topic by stating that the purpose of composition was just to 'get a decent grade'. At this point, he gave me a rather lopsided smile, cocking his head to one side and laughing. He did not appear to want to continue this discussion about the possible meanings his music had for him, signalled by the sudden change from a serious tone to one more frivolous as his banal final comment illustrates. The only boy who openly expressed that his musical ideas were connected in any way to self-expression was Edward from Old Tech Grammar:

> VA: So, do you prefer to have an idea given to you or use your own idea?
> Edward: Come up with my own.
> VA: Why's that?

Edward: Um, it just feels more a part of me. Um, yeah, I think it's a way of expressing yourself. It's a nice feeling to know you've just created something that sounds nice. (A level boy, Old Tech Grammar)

Certainly none of the other boys in the study ever suggested that the reason for using their own musical idea was connected to being 'part' of them. Edward's candour and readiness to discuss his music as self-expressive seemed even more anomalous as he was a pupil from Old Tech Grammar, where a particularly technological masculine identity was valued; a technological masculine identity that carried considerable status for male pupils and male teachers. Although the standard of playing amongst pupils at Old Tech Grammar was generally high, Edward was an extremely accomplished player (I heard him play the trumpet during a lunch-time jazz band rehearsal), having achieved Grade 8 Associated Board in both trumpet and violin. Although he stated that he quite enjoyed composing, he saw himself more as a player, being a very active member of the school orchestra and jazz group, and a member of the local youth orchestra and jazz band, which rehearsed on Saturdays. What set Edward apart is that he showed no interest in developing the highly prized technological identity sought by the other boys at Old Tech Grammar: he never used the music studio and, although I saw him composing at the computer during all of my observations (as was expected at this school), he never participated in any overt technological interactions with any other pupils or his teacher. Despite this, he still had considerable status within his peer group, who mentioned him as a being 'a really good musician' and as someone who could 'really play the trumpet'. The emphasis on playing traditional instruments in school music has often marked it out as a feminine subject, and boys who study school music often reject classical forms. However, it has been argued that those boys who are *expert* in the classical realm are able to transcend the gendering of school music as female through the appropriation of the 'higher-status' aspects of school music, such as composing, using computers or being an accomplished instrumentalist, all associated with males and masculinity (Green, 1997). Edward's rejection of a digital technological identity could be seen as an interesting example of this. Presenting himself as an expert classical musician allowed him to construct an alternative but equally 'successful' masculine identity because he excelled in this 'high-status' aspect of school music, a form of expertise particularly prized in this high-achieving school. As such, openly declaring that working with his ideas served the purpose of self-expression did not bring with it any possible fears that this might denote femininity.

Green's (1997: 215) study describes similar comments about boys' and girls' relationships to composition, which she suggests 'participate in an overarching discourse on masculinity and femininity'. Masculinity is characterized by 'a confident rational approach to composition based on creativity and genuine attainment through natural talent', while femininity is characterized by a lack of confidence in composition, which may also be bound up with feelings and self-expression. As the comments made by the female pupils indicate, the personal, expressive aspects of composing are important to their sense of self; an aspect of composition that the boys claim they do not feel. Citron (1993: 57–8) is curious as to why women have continued to compose given their lack of confidence and ambivalence towards composition. She speculates that 'composing may function for many female composers as a prime means of self-expression ... the main way to channel their inner selves into some tangible form', and that this may be different for men, who have more outlets for self-expression in Western culture. She goes on to suggest that, for women composers, this may bring the body and mind together, 'thereby resisting the negative implications of the mind–body split'. Green (1997), however, suggests that girls' references to self-expression and feelings of inadequacy as composers actually participate in the patriarchal definition of femininity precisely because feelings supposedly emanate from the female body and not the masculine, rational mind. When boys refute any connection of feelings with their compositions and present themselves as confident composers, this reinforces the construction of masculinity as cerebral, creatively autonomous and being in control of the body.

Deviance and conformity

In addition to these pedagogic concerns outlined above, my findings suggest that providing pupils with a musical idea can also have highly gendered connotations due to the extent to which boys and girls either conform or deviate from such stimuli supplied by teachers and circumscribed by examination syllabi. Whereas male pupils' 'deviance' is accommodated and encouraged by the teachers, female pupils are not always accorded the same degree of autonomy. Interestingly, as the above discussion shows, the issue of providing musical ideas elicited uniformly negative comments from virtually all the pupils interviewed, but the way in which they dealt with having to incorporate the stimulus or choose to deviate from it and teachers' gendered attitudes towards 'deviance' when applied to the work of boys and girls were markedly different. Green (1997) has also noted that both boys and girls prefer 'free composition', but the nature of examination syllabi and pedagogical models means that providing an initial compositional stimulus is common practice. Certainly, many of the classroom compositions discussed throughout this book originated from a teacher's musical idea or were strongly framed by syllabus requirements. It has been suggested that boys and girls respond differently to set tasks, with boys far more likely to deviate from given tasks. This has been interpreted by teachers as indications of boys' 'brilliance' and 'creativity', whereby girls' conformity is viewed as mere 'rule following' and shows their possible lack of real understanding (Clarricoates, 1978; Askew and Ross, 1988). The responses of Green's (1997) music teachers also viewed girls as more likely to stick to the given task, which ultimately led to the perception of them as more traditional and less imaginative. Arnot and Weiner (1987) have suggested that girls are more likely to avoid situations that hold the threat of failure, so if 'sticking to the task' is perceived as a prerequisite for 'success' girls are more likely not to deviate from what has been set. Consequently, conformity and passivity become part of an expected and acceptable femininity.

Assertive and disruptive behaviour by girls is likely to be viewed negatively, with both teachers and pupils tending to be more censorious. It has been observed that when primary schoolgirls tried to subvert traditional forms of femininity teachers labelled them 'real bitches' or 'little cows', suggesting that feminine 'deviance' is framed rather differently from masculine 'deviance' (Lakoff, cited in Reay, 2001). Francis (2000) notes that while both boys and girls can take up the position of 'class clown', using humour to amuse the class or as a way of resisting a teacher's authority, boys' banter was more likely to be tolerated by the teacher, who would occasionally join in and laugh at the boys' clowning around. Walkerdine (1990) also observed in her study of gender in the mathematics classroom that not only is boys' bad behaviour often downplayed by teachers, but 'being naughty' is turned into a positive attribute linked to an assumption of masculine creativity whereby boys are seen as 'independent, brilliant, proper thinkers', unlike girls, who are 'described as lacking the qualities boys possess. They are no trouble, but then their lack of naughtiness is also a lack of spark, fire and brilliance' (1990: 127). Green (1997: 200) makes a similar observation in relation to music composition 'where feminine conformity is taken to be a symptom of a lack of compositional ability and a dull musical mind, whilst, conversely, masculine non-conformity is understood to be a source of inventiveness and creativity'. It is precisely *because* boys play wrong notes, do not stick to set forms and 'experiment' more that teachers perceive them as having more imagination and compositional ability compared to girls. Girls are perceived as better at 'getting down to work' and tend to work harder, but this is given as a causal explanation for their lack of autonomy and creativity (1997: 198). Girls' qualities (of working hard and being quiet) are unfavourably compared to the creative and inventive qualities teachers attribute to boys that make them successful at composition. As one teacher commented, girls are more interested in 'writing things down and getting it right' but boys 'would rather be creative and not bother learning how to write/record work' (Green, 1997: 197).

In contrast, my findings did not discern a clear-cut gender divide between those who deviate from the task and those who adhere to it; there were examples of both boys and girls adopting this strategy. However, greater numbers girls at New Tech Comprehensive and Old Tech Grammar asserted that they retained the teacher's stimulus compared to girls from Arts College and Crossways Independent, who were more likely to assert that they would try to change or adapt the teacher's stimulus. As I argued in Chapter 3, the gendered discourses in operation in the four schools indicated a high level of variation regarding the prevailing processes and practices which, in turn, circumscribes pupils' perceptions of gendered expectations and behaviours, and what is or is not permissible or possible. Girls who stated that they would try to deviate from the task often referred to this more in respect of making it sound better, and it was noticeable that female pupils from

Old Tech Grammar and New Tech Comprehensive were far less likely to discard the stimulus entirely, a reluctance often expressed as lack of confidence in their own ideas:

> VA: If you are given an idea, do you feel you have to stick to it?
> Nina: I do largely stick to it because I haven't got much confidence to move away, to develop it on my own. I feel confident if I like my idea, if I think it's good structurally and it follows like rules. Yeah, but I do like it, I do prefer to stick to somebody else's idea. (A level girl, Old Tech Grammar)

> VA: Do you prefer starting from an idea that's your own or do you like to have something given to you?
> Gemma: Yeah, an idea which he's given us, the teacher. It's a starting point cos if you're told to just compose anything, yeah, it's a lot harder. I was given a chord pattern and then composed a melody over the top and I really enjoyed that cos I could hear it working and fitting together but when I sort of start completely blank, nothing to go from, I don't enjoy it cos I'm not getting anywhere. (GCSE girl, Old Tech Grammar)

> VA: If you've got an idea from the teacher, do you tend to stick to it?
> Laura: I think I stick to it quite a lot. Maybe just change the odd chord I suppose. (A level girl, New Tech Comprehensive)

In contrast, significant numbers of boys from all four schools were adamant that they would deviate from the given stimulus whenever possible and exhibited none of the girls' reservations about finding it hard to generate their own ideas. Dean, a young guitarist from Arts College with very little formal musical knowledge and limited music-reading skills (according to his class teacher), stated that he could not work with ideas he did not like and was keen to show that he could control and subvert whatever task was set:

> Dean: I can read music all the time, but I don't. I can play the piano but I just don't like it. I just find it a horrible instrument and I can't play something I don't like or do something I don't like. If I've already got something in my head I can't write [to a given stimulus]. Like I done a composition in school. It was supposed to be a sonata thing but mine was a rock thing. I made a song up on that. That was pretty good.
> VA: But if it was a sonata…?
> Dean: Well, there's no sonata things for guitar, but I could get round it. (GCSE boy, Arts College)

As described in Chapter 1 regarding the participating schools' characteristics, Dean was typical of the GCSE boys at Arts College, the majority of whom did not take formal instrumental lessons, often played drums or guitars, and were largely self-taught. Although self-taught pop musicians are often very highly skilled, the degree to which they are familiar with or use conventional staff notation varies considerably (Green, 2002). While sonata repertoire for the guitar is not extensive, it certainly exists and Dean's assertion that he 'got round' the 'sonata thing' because of the absence of this repertoire may in fact reflect his lack of confidence in his ability to tackle such repertoire. Rather than admitting that he may have experienced difficulties working from a given stimulus, this was instead framed within the view of himself as being original and free-willed, and is typical of an identity boys were keen to invoke, as is further illustrated in the comments below. Certainly, deviance is never framed as being linked to possible theoretical or musical deficiencies:

> Patrick: I'd be happier with that [own musical idea] cos I'd do what I want to do. It would sound better. Otherwise, I'm doing what he [the teacher] wants to make it sound right. Sir knows what it sounds like but we don't. We can't imagine the piece, what it sounds like. (GCSE boy, New Tech Comprehensive)

> Robert: I'm sort of free-willed I like to do what I want and I can't really seem to do something if I'm just given it. (GCSE boy, Old Tech Grammar)

> Steve: I would probably adapt it, change it to fit how I would do it because otherwise it's just inputting someone else's work. (GCSE boy, Old Tech Grammar)

Green (1997: 206) observed that boys expressed their negativity towards aspects of composition not in terms of lacking confidence or understanding but as their opposites. One of her male respondents stated that the reason he was not very good at composing was not through lack of ability but due to the fact that he knew so many 'famous tunes', and this specialist knowledge got in the way of his composition. This is similar to Robert's claim that his inability to work with an idea is connected to his identity as a 'free-willed' and independent thinker.

Accommodating deviance

There is evidence to suggest that when boys do deviate from the music stimulus they are more likely to go unchallenged, thereby affirming assumptions about boys' supposedly greater creativity and imagination as composers. The teacher's acceptance of their deviance appears to feed back into the boys' perceptions of themselves as creative, musically autonomous individuals and becomes, in Green's (1997) terms, affirmatory of their masculinity. This was certainly borne out in the ways that boys' and girls' deviance was perceived and accommodated by the teachers within my study. This flexibility was mostly in evidence (to varying degrees) at Arts College and Crossways Independent, and female pupils at these two schools said they felt able to be flexible in their approach to the set task and expressed the confidence to do so. Lisa from Arts College was a confident and enthusiastic composer and performer who, when asked if she was interested in composition said:

> Lisa: I love all of that! It's the thought of being able to make up your own type of mood, type of song or something. It's just, I dunno, it just appeals to me a lot. I'm definitely doing A level music. *(GCSE girl, Arts College)*

Lisa stated that she would 'get rid' of any ideas that she did not think were good enough. She said that she was happy to incorporate her own ideas with those of the teacher by taking out the 'best bits' suggested by her teacher and re-working them and, from her comments, this approach seemed to be not only accommodated but openly encouraged by her teacher, Miss Ellis:

> VA: When you've got an idea from your teacher, do you stick to it?
> Lisa: It depends what type of idea. If it's like a really good idea, I won't like to play it exactly how it is cos I wouldn't feel right about that so I'll take the best bits of it and kind of fiddle around with them slightly. It doesn't sound, it sounds slightly like it but it's got a bit of my own touch on to it. But if it's like not a very good idea, if I think it's plain or boring, I'll usually just get rid of it and make up my own. She'll [Miss Ellis] give you the ideas if you're stuck or she'll just say 'you could do this, this, this' and she always gives you lots of ideas so you don't just have the one for the whole class to work with.
> VA: Right.
> Lisa: And you've usually got a lot of leeway for you to change them around.
> (GCSE girl, Arts College)

Robert, a GCSE student at Old Tech Grammar, and a very confident user of technology (he nominated himself as the technological expert in his class; a role confirmed by his classmates in their questionnaire responses, and discussed in some detail in Chapter 4), asserted that he could not compose if he was given an idea because 'it sort of like pressurizes me. It's like saying you *have* to do this'. His strategy was to completely subvert the nature of the task that was set and, despite some initial misgivings by the teacher, he was allowed to continue to write what he wanted – also alluded to by Gemma, another pupil in Robert's class working on the same task:

> VA: Do you stick to that [the musical idea] or do you try to change it?
> Robert: I have an example of that. He [Mr Clarke] gave me, gave everyone this piece called 'Summertime' and we had to do an arrangement of it and um, mine was not 'Summertime' at all by the end of it. It's now like a sort of a club-dance remix style thing which he didn't like very much. He wanted to hear the actual tune but I'd changed every bit of it: the tune, the rhythm. He tried to make me

re-do it but no-one else re-done it so I didn't re-do it. (GCSE boy, Old Tech Grammar)

VA: If you're given a stimulus, do you tend to stick to it?
Gemma: Yeah, if it was like, well we did I think it was 'Summertime'. We had to do a variation on it and that I enjoyed cos it was, you had like a bass to go from and you just add bits in and take bits but play around with bits. But I stuck to the general thing, like 'Summertime', some people completely changed it but you weren't supposed to. (GCSE girl, Old Tech Grammar)

Gemma does not deviate from the brief given by the teacher and unquestioningly accepts his instructions, sticking to the pre-existing structure because that is what is expected. Robert, on the other hand, uses the idea of stimulus and the concept of an 'arrangement' very loosely and, even when challenged by the teacher, he refuses to change it. I asked Mr Clarke about this during his interview. He stated that, 'No, it wasn't what was set and I didn't really like it but Robert is very creative and he tends to produce really good pieces'. The teacher's perception of Robert's deviance (both musically and in terms of attitude, by refusing to acquiesce to the teacher's instruction to re-write his composition) becomes a sign of his creativity and, furthermore, his deviance is tolerated because his music is accorded *value*. As such, 'deviance' and 'value' enter into the discursive construction of masculinity but are not part of the discursive construction of femininity characterized by conformity and diligence, and as being non-innovatory (Green, 1997).

Deviance and musical value

These discursive gender constructions, when applied to the music classroom, not only define the level of teacher interference (as opposed to assistance) in a young composer's compositional process, but also define whose work is accorded value. I will attempt to illustrate this conflation of deviance with musical value by drawing on a detailed example of a similar situation at Crossways Independent in relation to Luke, a Year 10 GCSE pupil and Carolyn, a Year 12 A level pupil. Initially, from the classroom observations it appeared that the level of flexibility in working with the given stimulus exhibited at Arts College was also prevalent at Crossways Independent. Having spent a GCSE lesson reviewing Indonesian scales, the class teacher, Mr Trevor, told the pupils to use the notes of the scales they had just been looking at as a starting point for their own Gamelan compositions, and the following exchange then took place:

The teacher says 'I'll let you into a secret, I wasn't sure how much I wanted you to know beforehand about writing a Gamelan piece'. Luke asks does he mean 'not being tied down?' The teacher says he wants them to be 'open to their own inspiration' […] Luke asks about the time signature; he wants to use 19/2 but then says he wants to write it in 19/4. He says he'll try it and the teacher supports this idea and says it will naturally subdivide into smaller blocks. (Field notes, first GCSE observation, 28 February 2003).

After the lesson Mr Trevor and I met in the staff room and I was keen to explore his views about pupils' compositional process. He stated that he believed in allowing the pupils as much freedom as possible and did not insist on them writing 'strict pastiche' of any particular type of music because it was better for pupils to 'play around and see what happens', as evidenced by his support for Luke's inclination to experiment with the rhythmic elements of the piece. On the surface, this seemed an extremely positive scenario. However, after carrying out further observations and interviewing the pupils, I began to realize that what I had witnessed was indeed the teacher's tolerance and accommodation of deviance, but that it was more likely to be accorded to male pupils.

Upon my introductory first visit to the school, when I first met the pupils, Mr Trevor pointed Luke out as 'an extremely good composer', informing me that both his parents were professional musicians and that Luke was very talented. No claims were made for Carolyn's abilities when I subsequently visited my first AS level class (also taught by Mr Trevor), but I found out that she had achieved an A grade for GCSE music in her previous school and had been awarded consistently high grades for her compositions. When asked if he had noticed any differences in the way pupils composed using music technology, Mr Trevor stated that he tried not to impose too many restrictions on pupils during the early stages of their compositions because 'The fewer rules I give them the quicker they work and also the better they work. I mean, this isn't true of everybody of course. I mean, it's absolutely true of the most gifted.' It was noticeable that, when applied to Luke, the 'rules' were exceedingly flexible both in terms of musical parameters and how he occupied his time. He was given a high degree of autonomy in composition classes, often not composing at all. His minimal compositional activity in class, although commented upon, was tolerated because he was seen as a gifted composer:

> Mr Trevor: Luke […] quite likes to be cool and waste his time on Friday afternoons and mess around and then basically produces fantastic pieces, you know […] I wish he would focus more during lesson time but, if he's composing and bringing the work in to show me so it's not so important that he should be actually visibly engaged in work on Friday afternoons. (Music teacher, Crossways Independent)

This teacher's attitude towards Luke played a very strong part in Luke's construction of himself as a gifted composer. He was also acutely aware that the teacher's tolerance of his slack attitude on Friday afternoons was connected with this:

> VA: When you do have a brief from the teacher, to what extent do you stick to it?

Luke: If I'm doing my own work then I'll stick to it exactly but I don't really, that's the only time I might [...] Well unless I do it and change it and then it sounds awful then I'll put it to how it originally was and I'll save it but normally I'll change it.

VA: You don't ever feel constrained by the fact that you've been given a melody or a harmony framework or whatever?

Luke: I'm not given a melody or a harmony because, I don't know, well, I think some people are but I'm not sure I'm expected to stick to it. I dunno.

VA: What do you mean?

Luke: Well, I don't think, I mean, apparently anyway I'm much further ahead than anyone in the class or the year for music so I dunno, I'm just kind of left to potter about and see what happens really. Yeah, I dunno really. If I find something that sounds really nice the teacher won't make me change it because it's not exactly what he wanted [...] I've also convinced him that playing the guitar during lessons is also a definition of work! (GCSE boy, Crossways Independent)

This last sentence refers to what Luke usually does in Friday afternoon lessons, and my observations (all carried out during the Friday afternoon double lesson) confirm this.

This scenario contrasts sharply with the teacher's attitude towards Carolyn. Composition was viewed quite favourably by all pupils at this school and, like Luke, Carolyn was a particularly keen composer, often working with her brother's sequencing software at home, and she appeared to be trying hard to forge a strong compositional identity. In her interview she expressed consistent and very clear ideas about the music she wanted to write. However, unlike Luke, Carolyn was not viewed as a particularly gifted composer by Mr Trevor, and he would often become frustrated with what he saw as her 'inability to move ideas forward':

Carolyn: Yeah, um, I'd say I'm really satisfied with the minimalist style but I feel a bit, with the song I wrote that it's sort of, not to be rude about the teacher but I sort of felt it went off in the direction that he wanted it to go in and not so much in the direction that I wanted it to go in. And I felt it's sort of come away slightly sounding like popular music mixed with a Renaissance dance which sounds slightly bizarre. I still like it but it's just I don't feel that it was really what I wanted to write.

VA: How did that happen?

Carolyn: I think it was just because, I've got to do a middle eight section of the composition and I think he [Mr Trevor] was trying to show me how to do this by doing this composition with me and I think it sort of, he had to kind of show me how to do certain things, [so] it meant that it went in a different direction. Um, I started with a very good idea for the song but then I hit a hard wall sort of thing. I hit a barrier and it's quite hard for me to get over that and that was the point at which the teacher's influence on the piece came in because he was getting quite frustrated that I wasn't getting on with this piece and I was finding it quite difficult getting on with the piece so he just went 'Well, do this, do that, think about the instruments coming in there' and giving me these ideas and I just went with them because I couldn't think of anything else to do. Um, and I think that meant that it came out sort of with quite a lot of his ideas. (A level girl, Crossways Independent)

Despite her best efforts, Carolyn was not afforded an autonomous compositional identity, unlike Luke. While teachers need to be on hand to provide advice and assistance, in this case, it appears that this tipped over into something more akin to teacher *interference*. This was rooted in the teacher's perception of Carolyn's assumed lack of ability and his significant compositional input into her piece prevented Carolyn from developing and showing her skills as a composer. Rather than offering her a range of possibilities about how to progress, he removed all possibility of compositional autonomy from her, asserting his own compositional ideas and identity on her work. The time and flexibility accorded to the compositionally gifted Luke was not equally accorded to the apparently non-compositionally gifted Carolyn.

Although the teacher stated that he was in favour of giving his pupils compositional autonomy, this was contradicted by his comments about two female GCSE pupils whom he described as being quite 'malleable' in their compositional ideas:

Mr Trevor: Yes and not only that, they will, once a finished object appears like it did six weeks ago and was not yet ready, they will allow themselves to be persuaded and take it back and reconsider it and in fact, the finished items, the reconsidered items are very, very good. In every way, there is no way you can fault them. (Music teacher, Crossways Independent)

When talking about the boys in the same GCSE class, Mr Trevor seemed to allow them far greater latitude for initiating and developing their ideas. Although the teacher acknowledged that Ian and Jerome were 'not quite there yet' compositionally, he stated that, 'For Ian, I just have to wait for it to click in and I know that he will because I think he's a very bright chap. Jerome suddenly switched on and really wanted to do this thing so I'm letting him do it on his own, to find out what he can do.' Their perceived intelligence and compositional ability, despite some acknowledged shortcomings by the teacher, afford Ian and Jerome time and autonomy to work on their pieces. Conversely, Mr Trevor's perception of the girls in this class was that they required greater levels of intervention, although both boys such as Ian and Jerome, who were 'not quite there yet' compositionally, were allowed to find things out for themselves and work at their own pace (even if this involved doing virtually nothing in class, as was the case with Luke).

During his interview, Luke asserted that he was not able to compose at school because he had a 'creative block'. He said he was currently playing around with a chord sequence at home for a 'much bigger piece than anything I've really tried to do before' that would be scored for guitar, double bass, string quartet and percussion. The teacher also commented on Luke's intention to write this 'ambitious' piece and was happy to let him work this out in his own time, even if this resulted in significant indolence on Luke's part during composition lessons. Citron (1993: 60) asserts that the musical education required to become a composer reflects ideologies about the kinds of training needed to produce certain kinds of music; the type of music that embodies the value of the musical canon and has tended to privilege 'largeness: more notes, more sound sources, more performers, more volume'. These large-scale works also require greater understanding of the technical knowledge of harmony and orchestration and they have historically been prohibitive for women composers, as the most common outlet for female composers has been the least technical and technologically demanding types of composition, such as for the solo voice (Green, 1997: 93). Luke's ambitions to write a large-scale piece appear to reflect this privileging of male knowledge, supported by the implicit value judgement from the teacher that informs his relaxed approach towards Luke's classroom activities. In addition, the teacher's attitude towards Luke evokes Battersby's (1989) description of the male creative genius of the nineteenth century who embodies the values of originality, authenticity and spontaneity. But, as she points out (1989: 15), this is an evaluative term whereby the 'genius' is judged valuable in terms of his contribution to art and culture, and these will be *male* standards on which judgements are made. These judgements also accord with the notion of 'professionalism' which comes with a number of assumptions about the identity of the composer – that the professional composer will be male as the presumed repository of knowledge and skill, requiring cerebral control (Citron, 1993).

The above discussion demonstrates how the material structures of the classroom control and circumscribe an important aspect of the compositional process, and the different implications this has for male and female composers and the production of musical ability, as Mr Trevor's observation illustrations about what Luke does (or does not do) in lessons:

> Mr Trevor: As long as he's here and kind of thinking about it and vaguely thinking about what everyone else is talking about then actually, well for an adult we would allow that to be a vital part of the process so why on earth should that not be for a fifteen-year-old (Music teacher, Crossways Independent)

Echoing Luke's appraisal of his approach to composition, Carolyn acknowledged that 'I generally have to sit down and think about what I'm gonna do' to work on new ideas, but this was perceived by Mr Trevor as her 'always leaving things to the last minute'. Although both Carolyn and Luke appear to work best when starting from their own ideas, requiring significant amounts of time to let ideas ferment, Luke is granted the privileges of an adult male professional composer because he produces 'fantastic pieces'. However, Carolyn, whose compositions the teacher does not consider particularly noteworthy, is not accorded the same status, and this has serious consequences for her identity as a composer, as this poignant comment illustrates:

> Carolyn: I'm one of those people who tends to go off in their own direction and I get quite passionate about going off in my own direction. I'm not, I don't really like being told that it has to do this or sound this so I'm finding it quite frustrating when you realize you don't really have much choice in it and that it has to this and that and so, dunno. I mean, the whole point of composition for me is letting out the creative side [...] and then I'm like 'But I didn't want to go in that way', so I found with my song, because that was setting a poem to music, putting it into a song and I went away and spent a lot of time thinking about the poem that I was going to put in and the main melody and how that was going to reflect the poem and the feelings I felt came from that poem and that sort of, I wouldn't say it got lost but it's not clear now, so I think that's quite disappointing. There's not really a lot I can do about it. (A level girl, Crossways Independent)

This detailed discussion of Luke and Carolyn mirrors the observations made by Walkerdine (1990) and Green (1997), as outlined earlier, suggesting that boys' deviance is viewed positively as a sign of independence and creativity. As Citron (1993: 45) observes, 'patriarchal society has captured the concept of creativity and deployed it as a powerful means of silencing women'. Carolyn has certainly been silenced: her 'very good idea' transmuted into something that was not hers, and neither she nor her ideas appear to be valued.

Conclusion

While it may be common practice for pupils to be provided with musical ideas as stimulus for their compositions, in addition to the pedagogical shortcomings of this approach outlined above, I have argued that this also has a gendered dimension. Teachers' normative constructions of masculinity and femininity play a large part regarding the extent to which pupils' deviance from set tasks is either supported or rejected and, while boys' deviance is admired and encouraged for its perceived 'flair' and 'creativity', girls' deviance is configured rather differently in accordance with cultural assumptions about femininity and conformity. It may well be that some girls are more willing to rely on the guidance of the teacher due to a lack of confidence in their abilities (Green, 1997). However, it is important to recognize that lack of confidence is not an innate aspect of feminine identity but *becomes* part of a musical feminine identity, constructed by teachers' gendered discourses of what constitutes a 'gifted' composer (who is invariably male) and which then reflects back, negatively, on to these young female composers.

Chapter 6
Computers as a Medium for Composition

Studies have shown that computer-based music technologies afford a range of compositional strategies which allow pupils to focus on structure and texture (Gall and Breeze, 2005; Mellor, 2008) or to explore and experiment with sound (Savage and Challis, 2002), while others examine how compositional strategies might be differently configured for pupils with and without formal music instrumental training (Folkestad, et al., 1998; Seddon and O'Neill, 2003). While providing useful insights into the compositional process all appear to concur in their assessment that music technology is an inclusive and flexible medium that can support a wide range of learning styles (Hickey, 1997) and offers all pupils the possibility of compositional 'success' (Savage and Challis, 2001; 2003) irrespective of their level of musical knowledge and training (Nilsson and Folkestad, 2005). The arguments put forward throughout this book would suggest that such a perspective too narrowly circumscribes what constitutes educational inclusion in the technologized music classroom. This chapter is therefore concerned with how the computer itself can become a barrier to composition because of its focus on technological rather than musical control and mastery in classroom cultures that privilege a technological masculinity. The construction of masculinity is not a simple reflection of a general masculine culture but is the product of efforts to construct networks of men and machines that exclude women and femininity (Hapnes and Sorensen, 1995). As Grint and Gill (1995) rightly point out, while we must not take for granted the idea that technology and masculinity go together, the gendering of technology remains pernicious, differently positioning males and females according to what technologies are in use, in which locations and for what purposes. Accordingly, in this chapter I suggest that a purely computer-mediated approach to composition is likely to favour those pupils who see themselves strongly reflected in a classroom culture that constructs certain pupils as expert and technologically skilled, and these pupils are likely to be boys. As illustrated in Chapter 3, the gendered discourses in operation in the participating schools tended to privilege males' technological contributions, whether through talk or through the types of software with which they engage and which are actively involved in the construction of male technological expertise, producing gendered discourses that exclude girls and limit opportunities for them to display their knowledge and expertise. As their technological contributions are accorded less value this can make it difficult for girls and female teachers to be similarly positioned as capable technologists or accomplished composers. This may have significant implications for those pupils whose sense of compositional identity is not bound up entirely with technology.

These observations have particular resonance in light of the claims made for new digital spaces as being potentially empowering and democratizing for women because of the possibilities it affords for the reconfiguration of identity through these technological unions. The arguments put forward in this chapter suggest that the opposite may in fact be the case. As I suggested in Chapter 2, appropriating Haraway's (1990) provocative 'cyborg' may do little to disrupt and reconfigure women's material, embodied technological interactions in musical encounters. The cyborgian image is not necessarily helpful when arguing for women's agency unless we consider with whom power lies when making decisions about digitally mediated music interactions. This is explored when discussing the technocratic approach to composition in evidence at Arts College and Old Tech Grammar, which compels all pupils to take on the mantle of 'musical cyborg'. Unfortunately, this is an identity that may not be as affirmatory or flexible for all pupils as is supposed within these schools, and I will examine how pupils adopt or reject this technological focus in their compositional practices, and the extent to which they are able to exercise agency in their working practices as played out in the socially produced environment of the gendered classroom. This chapter offers an alternative reading to those authors who present unproblematic accounts of computer-mediated composition as being able to support educational inclusion, but from which discussions about the gendered nature of technological interactions are largely absent.

Technological mastery versus musical mastery

The designated space for composing at Old Tech Grammar and Arts College was in the music technology suite, where all pupils were expected to work at individual computers connected to a MIDI keyboard. Opportunities for working in a non-digital environment during lessons were not provided, and neither were there alternative spaces available for this. Boys' identities at Old Tech Grammar, Arts College and, to a lesser extent, New Tech Comprehensive were more overtly bound up in discourses of technological knowledge, and the most highly prized form of masculinity in these schools was materially and symbolically associated with skill, expertise and a supposed interest in all things technological. This results in a culture in which composing with computers is more likely to affirm boys' sense of identity in ways that are not available to female pupils. As such, boys are less likely to reject this technocratic focus or express any sense of alienation or disjuncture when working via this medium. Consequently, computer-mediated composition may result in a shift towards technological mastery and control, attributes culturally associated with masculinity, which means that boys are far less likely to experience this interruption in their construction of themselves as competent technologists and, by association, composers in an environment which enables them to construct an affirmatory masculine identity in this computer-mediated compositional culture. Expected to be competent technologists, boys' comments did not suggest that technology was perceived as an obstacle to composition, rather that they were inclined to assert that the technology was fully incorporated into their working practices, using it as an interactive medium throughout in ways that were integral to the process (Folkestad, 1998):

> VA: Do you ever compose away from the computer?
> Peter: No. I just do everything on computer really. I just find it much easier. I put ideas on the computer first and then, if it sounds wrong then I'll change it. (A level boy, Crossways Independent)

> VA: So do you put things straight into the computer?
> Edward: I find it a lot easier on computer cos if you make a mistake doing it by hand you've got to do it again.
> VA: When you're told to do composition where does that take place?
> Edward: Well, when we do composition we're in the music tech room.
> VA: Are you happy with that?
> Edward: Yeah. That's where I work best. (A level boy, Old Tech Grammar)

> Steve: I do that on computer. I just mess about with, put something in and then slowly do the other parts. (GCSE boy, Old Tech Grammar)

Despite the implicit assumption that music technology provides an egalitarian backdrop to composition, the ongoing masculine connotations associated with technology remain intact. Equating mastery with masculinity has also been attributed to men's apparent compositional 'success'. Reproducing the gendered discourses which link composition to the masculine mind and rationality, the nineteenth-century music critic Upton (Neuls-Bates, 1982: 209) claims that men are better able to master 'theoretical intricacies, the logical sequences, and the mathematical problems, which are the foundation principles of music', because this level of mastery and control is not available to women, who are too easily ruled by their emotions to be able to write 'great' music. Within the music classroom, similar discourses are in evidence producing an environment which reinforces traditional notions of masculinity and encourages a technologically focused approach to composition which may not be conducive to female pupils' compositional processes. Only one female pupil stated that, given the choice, she would still go to the computer first when working on a piece. This was the same (and only) girl I had observed working at a computer during my visits to New Tech Comprehensive:

> VA: Tell me about any particular likes or dislikes you have with respect to music technology.
> Alice: About using the computers, I think it's quite good how you can like play something in and then it'll write it down. It's easier to work with computers

because they have like many different tracks and things. Normally I write a
piece and go to the computer straight away to start it.

VA: Does that mean you have ideas before you go to the computer or do you go
there completely cold?

Alice: Go there completely cold. If I'm stuck I'll go to the computer and try and
start it.

VA: Can you describe how you go about working on a piece?

Alice: I guess I very much compose on the minute. I just sit there and whatever
comes into my head, I'll do it and then get it written down, get it played and then
get all my ideas sorted out and work on them all later and then, um, occasionally
if there's something not quite right about it I'll have to go home, I'll plan for
a couple of weeks, I'll go back and do it all over again just like sit there and
whatever comes into my head just play it, record it, have it done. (GCSE girl,
New Tech Comprehensive)

Alice was very much an exception, as girls were more likely to state that they
did not like having to use the computer during the initial stages of working through
ideas, and were unlikely to use the computers in school. Although they liked the
practical benefits the software afforded such as immediate playback, unlike Alice,
they reported finding it difficult working directly onto the computer while trying
out initial musical ideas:

Karen: I think it's better to use the computer when you've come up with the
basic melody or whatever and then you can elaborate on it but to come up with
original ideas it's easier for me to come up with something on the piano. (GCSE
girl, Crossways Independent)

Laura: It's good because you can actually hear what you're thinking straight
away. You get to hear exactly how you want it instead of the way you sort of
play it on the keyboard.

VA: Did you put the ideas straight into the computer at the very beginning?

Laura: No. I don't think I'd've got very far doing that.

VA: Why's that?

Laura: I don't know. It's just easier at the keyboard. You can play what you want
and when you're at the computer you have to have a bit of an idea to start with.
If it was just like a first little thought then it's as easy to write it down and then
I can think about it a bit more and then go to the computer. (A level girl, New
Tech Comprehensive)

This computer focus means that, in order to gain control of the sound and
the musical materials, pupils must first and foremost be adept at developing and
exhibiting *technological* skills where mastering the software becomes paramount.
Working in this way at the outset may mean paying less attention to the musical
qualities of their work, instead having to address the technical elements required to

realize their ideas. In the comments above, composition appears to be less concerned with musical mastery and more concerned with the notion of technological control and mastery, a shift that may act as a barrier to compositional 'success'. Girls were far more circumspect about what technology could help them achieve musically. Where music technology remained central to the compositional process, several girls commented that the purely musical aspects of their work were hindered because they had to focus solely on the technical aspects of the process:

> Laura: I think, when you're using the computer you don't think quite so musically. It's more sort of technical than the actual musical aspects of it.
> VA: Do you think that using music technology is generally a good thing for you?
> Laura: It helps me carry on but not to start with. I don't think it should be used for everything. You've got to have thoughts and stuff first of all and then use it. (A level girl, New Tech Comprehensive)

> VA: What do you like or dislike about music technology?
> Lisa: I like that fact that you can play more things on computer, but there's parts of it, like, cos I'm a piano player I can't pedal on the keyboard. It's certain things you can't do. It's a bit unmusical. (GCSE girl, Arts College)

> Nina: Yeah, I do tend to improvise, cos I do jazz piano and that helps a lot.
> VA: Do you think you could talk me through what you think are the good and bad points about music technology?
> Nina: Well, it does get in the way of what you want to do musically cos it's one thing playing it all out on the piano and it's another thing transferring it on to the score and making it sound like … You'd probably have to simplify it a lot more because it's just too complicated to put in. (A level girl, Old Tech Grammar)

> Carolyn: Positive aspects are it saves you having to write everything out lots and lots of times. Drawbacks is, it took me a few weeks to get used to it and I think that sort of took time away from when I could have been getting ahead with the composition generally. There are times when I find it quite frustrating because, it's like little things. If you have to spend five extra minutes trying to get the note to move you get wound up by it but maybe that's probably just me using it [laughs]. Possibly I'm not quite as good as I thought! I don't know, I found it hard to begin with because I found it stifled the whole creative process behind composition just because I had to learn how to use it and I had to learn how to use it to the best of my ability but while trying to compose at the same time. (A level girl, Crossways Independent)

This suggests that, when given the choice, girls do not automatically choose to work with technology but tend to approach the computer when they have a particular strategy in mind for how they intend to approach a given task, in contrast to boys who start working at the computer straight away, using a process of trial and error to carry out a particular task. This means that some pupils may find it difficult to construct a compositional identity that can move beyond that of technological controller and this can be particularly problematic for girls.

Turkle (1984) has called this controlled, structured way of working with computers 'hard mastery'. Although there is a degree of flexibility to 'getting it right', computational elements, abstract entities and the controlled use of the computer allow few possibilities for chance happenings. She asserts that the 'hard' mastery style, concerned with formal, planned thinking, is given privileged status and is a style sometimes (but not exclusively) associated with males and many computer-assisted learning sites due to the masculine culture in which these activities often take place. McCartney (1995) makes a similar observation with regards to electroacoustic composition, noting that particular kinds of equipment may encourage particular ways of working, based partly on the symbolic language used, type of interface, the shape and feel of the instrument and the assumptions programmed in to how the software will be used. This perpetuates what Murray (1993: 78) sees as masculinity's 'search for a controllable world of secure, certain and maintainable boundaries' through which 'technology legitimizes and makes "natural" binary ways of thinking and an obsession with planning and certainty'. Consequently, a classroom culture that emphasizes technological control as central to the act of composition may act as a barrier to girls' composing:

> Joanne: I do [compose for fun] occasionally, although not so much any more cos all this technology has really put me off composing. (GCSE girl, Old Tech Grammar)

> Nina: I tend to compose on the piano because you muck about with it more, you can manipulate it more but then the problem is transferring it on to the computer. You've got to find a rhythm and all that and I do find it easier but it's hard to make it sound like it on the computer because of, yeah, the different rhythm [...] Using technology's a whole lot harder and I'm struggling. (A level girl, Old Tech Grammar)

> Gemma: I find composing difficult anyway. Then with the computer I find it impossible. With the computer you have to put it in and then you think it doesn't sound right but you can't work out what sounds wrong cos whenever we're composing we're expected to do it straight on to the computer. I mean we've never sat in there [main music room with keyboards and headphones] and been told to compose. We're always told to go into the ICT room and compose on to the computer. With the piano, you can just kind of sit there and play something and keep altering it but with the computer you have to put it in and then you think it doesn't sound right but you can't work out what sounds wrong and you don't know how to change it. (GCSE girl, Old Tech Grammar)

These comments show how determinist assumptions underpinning educational policy are also played out in the classroom whereby computer-mediated approaches to learning are deemed beneficial to all students equally. As Bromley (1998: 2) asserts such a perspective is 'of dubious validity' because technologies 'partake in an epistemology that promotes certain visions of knowledge and notions of who counts as a knowing subject'. Therefore, learners who wish to make a choice about the extent to which technology is incorporated into their work and which media they work with, may find their apparent 'rejection' not only perceived as lack of interest but also interpreted by others as lack of skill and ability. As demonstrated in Chapter 3, this can result in girls in particular being excluded from technological talk and interactions that, when engaged in with teachers, marks them out as technologically expert.

Furthermore, this focus on the technological can also result in music that is unplayable and unidiomatic, a common problem when using music technology as a notational tool (Ofsted, 2009), and yet this is framed as one of the valuable affordances of music technology which supposedly offers all young composers wider creative possibilities: no longer are pupils limited to compositions they can play themselves, remember or notate; they can 'produce compositions that verged on unplayable on acoustic resources' (Mills and Murray, 2000: 141). Although this may indeed open up interesting sonic possibilities, the uncritical assumption that this is a positive aspect of computer-mediated composition for all young composers is not echoed in pupils' experiences:

> Carolyn: I also found that it ended up with me composing things that possibly I couldn't play because you could hear they sounded good on the computer but, that threw me a bit. (A level girl, Crossways Independent)

Alternatively, Steve and Craig's attitude to this aspect of their computer-mediated compositions appears less problematic as their music is not meant to be played. The music is conceptualized as fully integrated with the technology in terms of how it is composed and how they intend it to be heard:

> Steve: Well, if it's on the computer I don't intend it to come out. That would just be a computer thing. (GCSE boy, Old Tech Grammar)

> VA: Do you then play it [song written by interviewee] live from the score?
> Craig: No, no. Um, we've never really played live anything; it's just something we do for fun at home, yeah. It's all MIDI [...] I did write a song. It was probably at the beginning of the year, I wrote the melody and I asked Will to write the lyrics and then, yeah.
> VA: Did you perform that live?
> Craig: No, we don't perform them. We just sort of put them into Sibelius and leave them just to listen to later. (A level boy, New Tech Grammar)

The ability to manipulate the technology in order to achieve the musical outcome is enough for Steve and Craig as neither intend the music to be heard or played other than via a technological medium, unlike Carolyn's musical intention. Here, even though she is pleased with the end result when played back via the software, this 'unplayable' piece is not a cause for celebration but of concern; the unlimited affordances of the software which Mills and Murray (2000) are so enthusiastic about are not satisfying for Carolyn. Her sense of musical pleasure is not only linked to writing a piece that *sounds* good when played back digitally but is connected to writing a piece that she is physically able to engage with. Exhibiting technological facility and manipulation is no substitute for an embodied engagement with the musical work for this young composer.

The pupils' observations discussed above draw our attention to how compositional computer cultures can place too much emphasis on domination, control and mastery, characteristics normally attributed to males but not females. This supports Turkle and Papert's (1990) assertion that one of the reasons girls stay away from computers is because they come to symbolize an alien way of thinking in a culture that privileges technological control and mastery. These girls associate the computer's compositional role with the technological rather than musical aspects of their work, reflecting Caputo's (1994: 89) concern that this has gendered implications (and huge educational implications regardless of gender) because knowledge that cannot be communicated in digital form might be devalued: technology emphasizes digital knowledge at the expense of experiential knowledge. As girls are socialized to pursue relational, analogic ways of knowing, they must unlearn these ways in order to be successful with technology, therefore 'girls are set up for failure on some level as they confront technology and are measured by a male norm' (Caputo, 1994: 89). This should not be taken to suggest that girls cannot use technology but rather describes an antipathy for particular *types* of engagement and working practices in a digitally mediated environment over which they have little control.

Exercising agency and choice in a digitally mediated music classroom

Much has been made of the democratizing potential in women's digital interactions where computer technology is constructed as offering an autonomous, individual environment in which new identities and social relations can be forged but, as I suggested in Chapter 2, these human–machine fusions may be little more than symbolic representations that do little do disrupt existing social practices. It is more likely that 'ICTs are generally applied to already existing social practices, and therefore their use is more likely to "improve" current practices, not stimulate new social organization' (May, 2002: 154). Therefore, it is unlikely that arguing for human–machine musical amalgams will be able to challenge masculinity's material and structural association with culture and technology in the technologized music classroom. I concur with Davis's (1997) assertion that, while the image of the cyborg is said to offer new ways of thinking about women in the digital domain, this can lead to an abstraction of the body from concrete social contexts that lead to a disjuncture between the symbolic and the material:

> Bodies are not simply abstractions, however, but are embedded in the immediacies of everyday, lived experience. Embodied theory requires interaction between theories of the body and analyses of the particularities of embodied experiences and practices. It needs to explicitly tackle the relationship between the symbolic and the material, between representations of the body and embodiment as experience or social practice in concrete social, cultural and historical contexts. (Davis, 1997: 15)

This need to critically explore the embodied experience of the act of composing was very much in evidence within the technocratic culture at Old Tech Grammar, which resulted in a very narrowly circumscribed approach to the compositional process, a process centred on working with computers in the music technology suite. Opportunities to exercise agency and choice in the process were removed as the following description of an A level composition lesson demonstrates. During this lesson Miss Prime was working with A level pupil Louise in the music technology suite; Louise was writing a vocal piece for several voices using the notational software Sibelius. The first part of the exchange involved Miss Prime asking her to explain how the voices were working in harmony, which she duly did, but suddenly Louise shifted the focus of the conversation, pointing out to her teacher the problems she was encountering with the layout of her piece. She complained that things kept 'shifting' and she was having difficulties lining up the parts, problems which were slowing her down and making it difficult for her to move on with the piece. Despite Miss Prime's emphasis on the actual music, Louise's focus was drawn towards the more banal aspects of having to successfully manipulate the software which she seemed to be struggling with but which were taking up considerable amounts of her time. After the lesson, I spoke to Miss Prime about this exchange and was informed that this was the first time Louise had ever fully incorporated music technology into a composition from start to finish (this was the second term in the first year of a two-year course), and she was finding it quite difficult. I asked why she had chosen to work in this way if it was so hard for her and was told that she *had to* because it was for her coursework. Miss Prime went on to say that was how their pupils were expected to do it as it reflected positively on the school because scores looked more professional: 'it's not good enough to hand-write stuff nowadays'. This comment produces a discourse of 'professionalism' explicitly linked to the music department's perception of itself as producing high-achieving pupils in which digital knowledge, technological skill and expertise are highly regarded. She concluded by saying, 'anyway, it's easier to compose like that', although Louise's comments during the lesson imply that this was not necessarily the case for her. Although Louise had grade 7 with distinction in both piano and violin, the department's approach to composition may reinforce

Caputo's (1994) assertion that when digital forms of knowledge are more highly valued this results in an ideology that positions those without this knowledge as inferior, hence the teacher's insistence that Louise become technologically expert in order to achieve the required semblance of 'professionalism' expected within this music department. Dickinson's assertion that 'music technologies … also moonlight as systems of both control and empowerment' (2001: 337) is certainly borne out in this example, where music technology is used as a form of control by the teacher to circumscribe Louise's working practices. There is certainly no sense of empowerment at Old Tech Grammar, where all possibility for personal agency is removed. Again, this alerts us to how damaging such determinist discourses can be when music technologies are presented as devoid of social context in which the pupil's embodied compositional experience is secondary to the technological sheen required by the school to enhance its appearance of professionalism.

The musical cyborg of popular imagination conjures up images of young composers effortlessly and enthusiastically embracing the creative possibilities of these digital technologies but, for Louise, technology was not enabling but constraining and disabling. Despite having the most modern facilities of all the schools in the study, this school offered least opportunity for flexibility and agency in the compositional process. This suggests that, while girls may be able to use technology, and interested in it, they may experience antipathy for particular types of engagement in this cultural landscape which limits both the mode of composition and the range of compositional identities available to them. As Hodges (2007: 173) asserts, 'ICT should be an enabler, facilitator and support appropriate curriculum activities rather than dictating methods, approaches and learning experiences'. This suggests that greater flexibility is required in the classroom regarding the extent to which pupils are expected to incorporate music technology into their working processes, at what point the computer is incorporated into the process and what opportunities are available for combining this with acoustic instruments when developing their musical ideas.

This supports my argument that teachers should take a more flexible approach to using music technology, and this was very much in evidence at Crossways Independent, where computer-mediated composition was the exception (particularly amongst the female pupils) rather than the rule, and where the teacher's attitude was very relaxed about pupils' working practices. This led to an interesting approach taken by the two GCSE girls, Karen and Kezia. Although both stated that they hardly ever used the small music technology suite (and were not observed doing so during my visits) they said that they did incorporate music technology into their work by using their 'demo' copies of the score-writing notational package Sibelius[1] at home to capture their ideas; the resultant

---

[1]   These 'demo' copies of the software can be downloaded free from the Internet. They have limited functionality because work cannot be saved, but they allow the user to input notes into a score, add text and dynamics and print out the resulting score.

score would then be printed out and this would provide the framework for their reworking and revisions at the piano during lesson time:

> Kezia is sitting at the piano in the second practice room. I go in and sit down. She has a computer-generated score on the piano to which she is adding inner parts by playing them on a piano. She says it's easier to play on the piano rather than clicking a mouse [a reference to the way notes can be inputted using Sibelius software]. She asks me to play the two upper parts so that she can hear them as she doesn't play piano very well. I play them and we talk about the intervals, some of which sound very dissonant, and she doesn't like them. I ask her to analyse what she's written. She then realizes why it hasn't worked. As a tuba player, she's more used to reading bass clef and has put the notes in the treble clef as if they were in the bass clef. (Field notes, second GCSE observation, Crossways Independent, 7 March 2003)

> Karen has written parts for xylophone and drums. She is adding parts to a computer-generated score she prepared at home. She says she will add chords on the piano by hand. I sit in the practice room and watch her trying out different chords. Having worked like this for about ten minutes, she asks me to play the xylophone part on the piano, while she plays the chords, so she can hear what she's written. (Field notes, third observation, Crossways Independent, 14 March 2003)

This approach, while appearing rather cumbersome and labour intensive, appeared to offer a satisfying combination of acoustic and digital methods. Even though inputting notes directly into Sibelius would have afforded the possibility of immediate playback (without the need for someone else to play additional parts), neither girl commented on this negatively. During their interviews I asked the girls about their low level of music technology use when composing. Although Karen said she mainly used it during lunchtimes and after school she said, 'it's easier to do it [compose] on paper'. Kezia had stated on her questionnaire that she was a confident use of technology, but she still made minimal use of the software for composing:

> VA: It looks like you don't use the music technology much [referring to her questionnaire].
> Kezia: Cos I don't really use it at school.
> VA: You don't?
> Kezia: I've got a demo at home which I use.
> VA: So how much time do you spend using it?
> Kezia: Um, only for homework really, about half an hour a week.
> VA: How do you feel about using music technology?
> Kezia: Good but I don't really use the computer that much. I've only just started using the computer really for my work. I've always done it by hand.

The culture at Crossways Independent was the least technologically oriented, and the teacher was quite flexible regarding the extent to which technology was incorporated into the process. As Karen commented about her teacher's attitude to whether or not they used computers, 'He's not really bothered, I don't think, as long as we're happy with the work we come out with in the end.' The piano played a large part in both her and Kezia's compositional processes. Ideas were worked out acoustically, and only when these had reached a certain stage in the process were they inputted into Sibelius:

> Kezia: So the first thing was the German poem he gave us. The chord pattern in the second piece was I–IV–V so he just set us the task to find a love poem and write a piece, and I went home and thought it would be nice to write for piano. It's a love song, and it's [the piano] a typical lovey-dovey instrument and soprano voice so, I took the first line which was 'My Mistress' eyes' and I just came up, just hummed a melody really. I worked out the notes on the keyboard and wrote them down and just carried on from there. I chose D major cos it was a nice happy chord and I chose to make the song happy because at the beginning it sounds sad but I wanted to build it up for the end, the happy end. I do modulate into the minor after I've done those four chords to get more tense because you think it's getting worse. In the end it goes back into major, D major to end happily and once I had the melody, I put the melody on to the computer at that point, so I could hear how it sounded. (GSCE girl, Crossways Independent)

> Karen: Yeah. Um, I prefer working at the piano. I find it easier to come up with things. Like with the piano I can just find a few chords and work from there I just find it easier. Um, well the one we just did was a song. So we had to find a poem, a love poem and which rhymed and then I picked a key signature and I did the melody, um, first to go with the poem, because, um, yeah I added the chords that used notes of the melody. I start with a few sort of notes, melodic ideas and then um, depending on the mood I'm trying to set up I sort of, I change it to suit the mood of the piece. I just build it up using layers and stuff. (GCSE girl, Crossways Independent)

Similarly, Lisa from Arts College also stated she was less likely to use the computers unless specifically instructed to do so by the teacher although, from the setup of the classroom and the observations I undertook, opportunities to work with just the piano were severely limited during lesson time:

> VA: So when you have the choice to use the computer or not what do you do?
> Lisa: I usually tend not to but if I'm on the keyboard I'll use it but if I get the chance to use the keyboard or piano, I'll use the piano […]
> VA: How do you play around with your ideas?
> Lisa: Cos I have a piano at home I usually play around for a bit at home and try to remember it and then, if we have to record it on to the computer I'll put it on

computer and then play around for a while longer at home and then bring it back
into school.
VA: You don't go straight on to the computer?
Lisa: Not unless we've been told to. (GCSE girl, Arts College)

What was significant was Lisa's marked delineation about the computer's
role in her process, and she actively sought ways to circumvent the technological
mantle forced upon her in lessons, separating out different elements of her process.
It is telling that she only works directly on to the computer when instructed to
do so. Like Kezia and Karen, it appears that her preferred mode of working is
more flexible and not wholly mediated by the music technology. These girls all
managed to develop working processes which allowed them some degree of
choice regarding the computer's role in their compositional process.

Conclusion

Where teachers' focus is on computer-mediated modes of working during
compositional lessons, they are likely to perpetuate an implicit assumption that
music technology provides an egalitarian backdrop to composition which will be
conducive to all pupils. However, as I aimed to illustrate in this chapter, this can
produce an environment which reinforces traditional notions of masculinity where
a technologically focused approach to composition results in the construction of
a masculinist culture which appeared to favour boys. My findings indicate that
boys tended to incorporate the technology more readily into all stages of the
compositional process and did not express any sense of interruption or feelings
of alienation in their working practices. While happy to incorporate technology,
girls were less interested in using it for the whole of the compositional process.
This is not to suggest that these young female composers were not interested in
using technology, but their use of music technology was highly judicious and
they often expressed a preference for the more 'lo-tech' end of the spectrum.
Where technology becomes the focus of the compositional process, I suggested
that girls might perceive this as a barrier to composition whereby technological
manipulation could sometimes override the musical concerns. To circumvent
this, ideas were often worked out on a piano or keyboard first and then played
around with acoustically before bringing technology into the process, but this
was not always possible given the inflexible working environment of two of
the schools, where composition was always carried out in the music technology
suite.

The need to encourage women to engage with technology is not being
questioned here, but we need to go further than just arguing for liberal
interventionist approaches. Uncritically embracing the march of technology will
change neither the material nor cultural constraints that women face in their actual
experiences of the technological world, but recognizing that women must be

afforded *material* opportunities to take control of and make choices about their technological engagement does have the potential to influence gender–technology relations and the gendered cultures in which technologies are used.

Chapter 7
Reclaiming Compositional Spaces

In the previous chapter I examined how boys and girls respond when expected to compose via a digital medium and I suggested that a technologically focused approach was more amenable to boys than girls. Girls were far more likely to seek alternative modes of composition that afforded greater levels of flexibility in their compositional processes, but I showed that they were often prevented from doing so in schools where composition was only ever carried out in the music technology suite. This final empirical chapter continues to explore the theme of flexibility through an examination of the spaces in which composition takes place. I believe that arguments suggesting music technologies can provide the possibility for meaningful and empowering interactions for women must remain focused on the *material* structures in which women engage with technologies. The symbolic representations of musical cyborgs critiqued in Chapter 2 may be powerful rhetorical devices but they are unlikely to disrupt or reconfigure the ongoing material connection between men, masculinity and technology. Unless women genuinely have control over their technological interactions, it is difficult to see how they can claim a positive feminine identity when engaging with technologies. This chapter is therefore concerned with the extent to which female pupils are able to exercise agency and choice when negotiating the digitally mediated compositional space of the classroom. As the reader will be aware, the study was carried out in the classroom, but it was striking that pupils' comments often referred to their compositional processes in the home. Therefore, it seems important to acknowledge this in my discussion as it appears to provide for greater levels of autonomy and choice in the compositional process that is sadly lacking in the classroom.

Gendering compositional spaces

While the construction of compositional spaces may impact on the choices available to the pupils, pupils themselves also have an important role to play in the co-construction of these gendered technological spaces. Space is commonly thought of as a fixed, physical container of social life, a place where things happen, but educational spaces are more than either a physical or social space and can be viewed as an interaction between the two; not as a backdrop to social interaction but created *through* interaction with the social and therefore socially produced and interpreted (McGregor, 2004). This helps us to understand the organization of space in schools and how it produces particular forms of social relations so that 'Rather than being an arena *within which* social relations take place, space is made *through* the social – it is enacted and so continually created and recreated' (McGregor, 2004: 2). As McGregor goes on to say, understanding space as socially produced reveals social arrangements which produce and maintain power relations whereby individuals and groups use space to exert dominance over others. Within classroom spaces, teachers lay down rules and routines controlling pupil behaviour, movement and access to technologies, and, in creating these structures, certain behaviours are encouraged or suppressed which function invisibly to reinforce teacher control (Coffey and Delamont, 2000). Ignoring how space makes a difference to schools and education is a barrier to democratic relationships because space is never neutral but is (re)created through politics and ideology and is actively constructed through materially embedded practices (McGregor, 2004).

Negotiating technological and compositional spaces

This highlights the need to take seriously the relevance of gendered social interactions to help us understand the construction of technological spaces in the music classroom and how it circumscribes the experiences of pupils working in these contexts. As Pegley (2000) argues, often insufficient attention is paid to the way music classrooms, as new technological spaces, are constructed because we focus too narrowly on the effects of computers on pupils' literacy and creativity rather than examining the gendered interactions that produce classroom spaces, a scenario that reproduces an overtly deterministic understanding of technology's apparent impacts. Exploring boys' and girls' interactive patterns in six technology 'locations' within the music classroom (literacy, sequencing, composing, MIDI wind performance, recording and integrated arts performance) she notes that the restructuring of physical space has a palpable effect on a pupil's sense of place within it. Boys' and girls' negotiative styles altered as their groups moved around between the different locations. Pegley makes the point that pupils' musical voices are shaped by their personal constructions of place, and these constructions are highly gendered. Girls were more likely to favour locations that involved less focus on manipulating computer software but encouraged personal interaction, whereas the boys appeared to favour more technologically oriented locations that featured individual activities (Pegley, 2000: 311).

As I pointed out in Chapter 1, there has been a discernible rise in the numbers of boys opting to take music in school, one of the reasons given being the greater use of technology, said to appeal more to boys' interests. Recent research suggests that this is echoed in UK university music departments where technology is the focus. As Whistlecroft (2000) notes, in universities where music technology was not a compulsory part of the course, women would often opt out, particularly from studio and composition work, and retention amongst women students was often low. It is noteworthy that the university with the most outstanding record of recruiting and retaining women in this area had four women on its staff of nine, including one composer. Often the spaces in which women are expected to compose can seem alien, and in order to be accepted within these masculine spaces women feel compelled to minimize outward appearances of femininity in order to fit into the 'macho' culture of the electroacoustic studio. Commenting on her experiences of studying composition in Canada, Gayle Young observed that there was only one female member of staff and one female student (her) on the composition course and she adopted a particular strategy in order to fit in:

> Being one of the boys was my way of dealing with it – I dressed like one too …
> I wore heavy workboots and huge T-shirts … Females students who can't easily
> fit in would do something else, just back out. (McCartney, 1995: 4)

My findings show a similarly gendered construction of space. At Arts College and Old Tech Grammar, all composition took place in the music technology suite. Crossways Independent also had a small music technology room but there were fewer computers in this department, as was also the case at New Tech Comprehensive, but throughout my visits the rooms in which the computers were located were consistently occupied by male pupils in these two schools. Incidences of female use were far fewer where choice of compositional location was available and, as discussed in the previous chapter, girls were more likely to be found in practice rooms, trying out ideas on the piano, and notating them down on manuscript paper, usually with a view to transferring them to the computer at a later date. When computers are situated in a very male-dominated environment, girls may feel less comfortable inhabiting such spaces as there is a perception that computer rooms are 'male' territory, an alien space in which boys' attitudes and behaviours tend to dominate (Culley, 1988), and this is particularly noticeable in the context of computer gaming. Watching a group of boys huddled round a computer playing a game called *Incredible Machine,* Orr Vered (1998) observed that the process of play was very loud and energetic. There was a lot of calling out and 'directing from the floor', a very cooperative form of play but nonetheless peppered with much noise and shouting. Of course, girls can be noisy too but the social context had a palpable effect on girls' willingness to play in this environment. They often watched but rarely actively participated in the all-male groups, leading Orr Vered to conclude that girls limited their participation to that of observer in this particular context. As one girl stated, 'they're always yelling at the people who are like wrong. And I don't wanna be yelled at because I don't wanna be wrong. 'Cuz like whenever I like think of an idea, and I like tell them, and then if I'm wrong, then they'll probably like start yelling' (Orr Vered, 1998: 55). If we ignore this gendered construction of space we are in danger of producing crude accounts of girls' lack of participation similar to that put forward by Cooper (2007) in her observation that lunchtime music technology clubs attract more boys than girls. As gender is never explicitly mentioned as a reason for not attending, this leads her to conclude that girls are not less capable but less interested in technology.

As a result, she may unintentionally reproduce the very gendered technological discourses she set out to examine.

What the above further illustrates is that where males have more power to influence the construction of technological locations as their own this can result in making these spaces 'off limits' to females. This highlights the material power relations produced in and around technological spaces, which were particularly overt at Old Tech Grammar. During her interview, Joanne had expressed an interest in using a particular piece of software that included audio input. She could not remember the name of the software but talked enthusiastically about it as she thought it would be helpful in her compositional process:

> VA: Right, so this audio software you were talking about, was that for instruments and voices?
>
> Joanne: Yes but I've never gone into all of that.
>
> VA: Oh, you haven't used it?
>
> Joanne: No, not really.
>
> VA: Why?
>
> Joanne: Well, that's in the studio generally and I don't go in there. (GCSE girl, Old Tech Grammar)

It transpired that this small recording studio was mainly used by four boys doing music technology A level (two were also studying for music A level, one of whom participated in the study). During my observations I came to understand how Joanne's perceptions of this space as highly gendered and 'off limits' prevented her from engaging with the different software available in there. I too was made to feel I was not welcome, as my unsuccessful attempts to gain entry to the studio testify. The first occasion occurred after the completion of the questionnaires on my first visit. Having collected the questionnaires and noted which A level boys had agreed to be interviewed, I went to find them in order to ascertain when their free periods were so I could start planning the interview schedule. Leaving the music technology suite, I glanced across the corridor and could see several of them through the window of the recording studio but, as I moved towards the studio door one of the boys walked towards me and stood in the doorway making it impossible for me to enter. I eventually had to take up a position just outside while they continued talking and laughing amongst themselves. Once I had ascertained which pupil had agreed to participate, the information required was politely provided but none of the boys responded to my subsequent informal questions about what they were working on. Feeling that I was interrupting and was not welcome there I left feeling uncomfortable at the position in which I found myself. This should not perhaps have been surprising as research has highlighted the cultural construction of the recording studio as a predominantly masculine domain (Sandstrom, 2000; Smaill, 2005), a site which excludes women, who are not expected to exhibit technical knowledge or expertise (Leonard, 2007). Attempting a second visit when there were only three boys in the studio thinking, perhaps somewhat charitably, that my inability to gain entry on the previous occasion might have been due to lack of space in this small room again proved futile. The physical positioning of the boys within the studio left me hovering in the doorway once more. The boys' physical and symbolic control of the space meant that even I, an adult visitor to the school, could not gain entry. Consequently, no further attempts were made to gain access to the studio.

This shed new light on Joanne's apparently commonplace statement about her lack of access to a particular piece of software saying 'Well, that's in the studio generally and I don't go in there'. I imagine that, given her even 'lowlier' status (as a GCSE pupil) than mine (as visitor and researcher) in the eyes of the male occupants of the studio, entry would have proved impossible but, in her case, it was rather more important that she gained access as failure to do so resulted in her not being able to develop her skills and extend her expertise in the use of different music software.

As I have noted previously in the book, at both New Tech Comprehensive and Crossways Independent girls were very rarely seen using the computers and at the former I only observed one girl working at a computer during all of my observations. When I asked Mr Yardley from New Tech Comprehensive how much technology was involved in his composition classes he said that his pupils rarely used it, stating, 'there's not much of a computer culture amongst the A level pupils although it's changing in the lower years'. However, the questionnaire responses revealed that two boys and five girls out of a cohort of thirteen A level students (three boys and ten girls) actually had access to music software at home. When I pointed this out to Mr Yardley he was very surprised to hear that half of the girls in his class were using music software at home, particularly as he perceived them as being very 'traditional' in their approach to music composition (all were classically trained with the exception of one self-taught female guitarist) and he had not thought they were interested in technology. It is worrying that, despite this teacher's assertion that there is not much of a computer culture in the music department, even at this very early stage of technological investment and use, the fledgling compositional culture is already constituted through male expectations of computer use and interests. Having noted that amongst his pupils it was largely the boys who tended to use the music suite most frequently during lessons and lunch hours, Mr Trevor from Crossways Independent nevertheless asserted that he did not believe this was actually a cause for concern. The problem as he saw it related to the need to increase music technology provision and have access to a dedicated technician, a not unfamiliar problem in secondary school music departments (Ofsted, 2009):

Mr Trevor: With the half-hearted technology we have at the moment we are not actually quite ready to have a culture [...] Look at the difficulties we've got even getting the basic requirements so the kids can get on to the computer and do music and stuff. (Music teacher, Crossways Independent)

When I pointed out that I had not seen any girls in the music technology suite during my observations, the teacher merely put this down to lack of access:

> Mr Trevor: It's certainly there in those classes where both genders are present so girls tend not to use computers when there are boys around to stop them using it, whereas they're [the girls] perfectly happy to use them if there's no one around […] I think as soon as we have enough hardware the problem will pretty much disappear. (Music teacher, Crossways Independent)

A similar opinion was expressed by Mr Yardley at New Tech Comprehensive:

> Mr Yardley: Yeah. The boys tend to use the computers a bit more. We don't have much of a culture of computers yet but that'll change when we get more money, probably next year, and access won't be a problem. (Music teacher, New Tech Comprehensive)

Although the teacher at Crossways Independent seemed to acknowledge that girls were less likely to use computers 'when there were boys around to stop them', he did not seem to think that this was particularly significant or problematic.

While the scenario at Crossways Independent could be viewed as girls exercising choice about their mode of composing, with so few computers and boys hogging both the equipment and the technological space, I would suggest that the notion of choice is rather more complex. Rather, it would appear that the absence of the girls from the small technology suite at Crossways Independent was linked to their reluctance to enter spaces identified as overtly masculine. Unfortunately, this can result in a further strengthening and alignment of technology with males and masculinity that teachers appear to accept as the norm – a few more computers is apparently all it will take to rectify any perceived gender 'imbalance'.

Reclaiming technological and compositional spaces

In the masculine sphere of technology, boys are said to dominate, but it has been suggested that this is not without its problems as boys are supposed to be knowledgeable about technology and may be anxious not reveal any 'lack' or deficiencies in their understanding. This can involve 'having constantly to secure their position in the public sphere because expertise in the subject content constitutes part of their identity' (Elkjaer, cited in Stepulevage, 2001: 329). Girls, on the other hand, as 'guests' in this symbolically masculine space do not have to secure their position in the same way as their gender identities are not bound up with having to display technological expertise, so it could be argued that similar pressures do not apply. Unfortunately, this can work against them in the eyes of teachers and other pupils who position them as apparently non-technological if not seen overtly engaging with technology, as evidenced by Mr Yardley's comment above about the apparently 'traditional' female A level students. As I demonstrated in Chapter 3, boys are more likely to secure their position in technological spaces through the types of talk in which they engage with male teachers and what they bring into school in terms of their informal technology knowledge and skills. This reflects Ofsted's (2009) observation that schools know virtually nothing about their pupils' prior musical experiences or interests. In this case, it can lead to teachers' incorrect and negative assumptions about their female pupils' level of engagement with music technologies, based solely on what happens in the classroom perpetuating gender 'myths' that serve to reinforce dichotomous distinctions which position girls as 'traditional' and apparently non-technological.

While, as I have shown, some girls are more circumspect in their relationship with technology and use it relatively infrequently in classroom spaces when they have the choice, there was a small group of girls who did incorporate music technology more regularly into their composing. What is particularly noteworthy here are the active steps they took to claim a *new* technological space for themselves within the context of the home. By choosing to use music technology at home rather than at school they appeared to circumvent the need to negotiate the overtly masculine space of the music technology suite which, as the teachers' comments above indicated, are often filled with boys:

> Joanne: I've had a lot of practice mucking about with it [compositional software] at home and I've got used to how everything works, which is quite useful. I mainly use it for coursework cos I don't have much time to do anything else.
> VA: Does that help?
> Joanne: Yeah. If I only used it at school I wouldn't be able to use it as much or get time on the computers so it would hinder me.
> VA: Do you prefer to work at home?
> Joanne: Yeah. It's quieter and you can spend, well because it takes a long time to do anything and because the periods are an hour you can't get much done whereas you can work like two hours at home without getting interrupted. (GCSE girl, Old Tech Grammar)

> Nina: I've got the Sibelius but it's the original version. So I do the bulk of it [composing] at home and then sort of tweak it at school in the lessons. (A level girl, Old Tech Grammar)

Despite the exceptionally high level of music technology access at Old Tech Grammar it is significant that many of the girls who stated that they were more inclined to use music technology at home were from this school, a school where male pupils and teachers were invariably constructed as the technological experts. The questionnaire data showed that of the fifty-four pupils who said they had access to compositional software at home only eighteen were girls, and there was a marked difference in the types of software they used. In line with my discussion of the gendering of music software put forward in Chapter 4, four girls had access to Sibelius, another four to Sibelius and Cubase, with the remainder using Music Time Deluxe or Cakewalk. In contrast, twelve boys used Sibelius, and seventeen also had Cubase and/or Logic software at home, with several pupils also using the software Reason, Fruity Loops or Cool Edit Pro, which none of the girls had at home.

We must still be mindful of the potential problems of claiming the 'private' space of the home as a celebratory site of female agency given that the socially produced nature of space is also a contested site for gendered social relations. Orr Vered (1998: 46) asserts that, in similar ways to the classroom, 'home is also a highly structured social space' circumscribed by rules and regulations, social relations among individuals that dictate access to technology, such as the computer or video recorder. Even where there are computers in the home, they are usually located in shared spaces such as dining rooms and so on and are not the sole preserve of young people, who usually have to share them with other family members. Therefore, computer use is likely to be a contested activity within the household (Facer et al., 2001) and so composing at home is not without its problems, as Joanne's comment illustrates:

> Joanne: I prefer to compose at home but as long as there's not lots of people around. It's not like in a quiet room of its own, it's in the living room and so if there's lot of people watching television I can't go in there. It gets a bit annoying. Sometimes, if I'm on my own or someone's upstairs, it's all right. (GCSE girl, Old Tech Grammar)

Boys are more likely than girls to have personal ownership of a computer (Facer et al., 2003) therefore, despite the physical location of the computer within the home, the meanings that are ascribed to it can continue to align it with the males in the household. This again highlights the arguments put forward in Chapter 4 regarding the gendered construction of technological expertise and skill, which serves to both materially and symbolically position females with technologies in ways that do not confer any form of power or expertise within the wider social framework. The home environment is therefore revealed as another social space involved in the production of a set of social relations in which masculinity retains its privileged position by engaging with *valued* technologies such as computers.

The comparatively high level of music technology use at home by girls was not anticipated in light of the classroom observations, although Holloway and Valentine (2003) note that girls who have access to PCs at home have the opportunity to develop technological competence away from 'surveillance' and the often 'hostile gaze' of their peers, and these girls inevitably become more confident users, a confidence that is not always reproduced in the classroom. Even so, girls appeared reluctant to show what they could do in classroom situations in case they encountered difficulties that revealed things they felt they could *not* do, which might expose them to teasing by the boys if they could not perform at the right speed or level. My findings suggest that, like the girls in Holloway and

Valentine's study, one of the ways female pupils circumvent having to negotiate the overtly masculine music technology classroom is to engage with music technology at home; a private space away from the glare of 'public' failure.

This is an interesting but potentially troubling finding, as this notion of 'public failure' could be interpreted as a highly essentializing positioning of these young female composers, which further reinforces the distinction between male/ female and public/private spheres, a distinction that many women, and women composers, have endured over the centuries (Citron, 1993; Reich, 1993; Halstead, 1997). Furthermore, given that girls have fewer opportunities to claim skills status in technological contexts (Faulkner, 2001) their exclusion from the more public masculine technological domain of the music technology classroom may further reinforce this gendered public/private divide. The cultural practices around composition have historically produced a symbolic, material and ideological distinction between the private 'feminine' sphere and the public, professional 'masculine' sphere, the latter held in greater esteem than the former. Historically, women's music is heard less frequently in public spaces, receiving far fewer public performances than their male counterparts, which Citron (1993) claims is significant because

> it is important to note that the gendered associations of public and private mean more than site, agency, and social status. They have important metaphoric and epistemological implications as well. They symbolize psychic space: women and private as reined in and bounded, men and public as free and open … Public represents an epistemological space without limits, and therefore privileged. Private suggests boundaries of knowledge and access to knowledge; it implies a lesser justification for knowledge and authority. (Citron, 1993: 104)

This 'reining in' of women in the private sphere has significantly contributed to female composers' exclusion from the musical canon (Citron, 1993; Solie, 1993; Cook and Tsou, 1994) as male composers regularly obtained public performances in contrast to their female counterparts, whose work was rarely performed in public or published.

When women composers and conductors do make it into the public domain, critics may be more concerned with their looks than their musical abilities (Halstead, 1997). This is nicely exemplified in an article in the magazine *Muso* (2005) which compared the careers of two up-and-coming young conductors. The article about the male conductor comprised a large picture of him which took up about one-third of a page while the remainder of page detailed his achievements, musical background and forthcoming engagements. He is seen wearing everyday clothes of a style that suggests the photograph may have been taking during a rehearsal, as he is holding a baton in his hand as if he were actually conducting. In comparison, in the article about the female conductor her image takes up the whole of the two-page spread, very much in the style of a 'centrefold', while her professional experiences warrant a few brief lines in the bottom left-hand corner of the picture. She appears to be wearing a white silk nightdress while lying on a white fur blank fully made-up with painted nails; artfully arranged hair hangs seductively over her eyes as she looks up at the camera. She appears to be more ready for bed than she is for conducting an orchestra, which is no doubt what the image hopes to imply. The sexual overtones implicit in this image are exacerbated by the salacious tone employed in the first paragraph:

> Estonian conductor Anu Tali heads the Nordic Symphony Orchestra, which she and her identical twin sister (now there's an image) founded together in 1995. (Muso, 2005: 38)

This demonstrates that, despite larger numbers of women successfully entering traditionally male-dominated areas of music, women's compositional and musical spaces continue to be circumscribed by societal expectations of women and patriarchal notions of what constitutes acceptable forms of femininity in these spaces. As the discussion above illustrates, the attributes worthy of note are differently configured for the male and female conductor: while the male conductor is presented as a 'serious' musician, the female conductor appears rather frivolous in comparison and, without reading the accompanying text, the reader would be hard pressed to deduce that here lay the founder of the Nordic Symphony Orchestra and a conductor of growing international repute.

Having highlighted the problems women musicians may face in the public realm I also recognize the apparent paradox of identifying the home as a site for female agency, associated as it is with the stereotypically 'feminine' activities of caring and nurturing, and shouldering the onerous burden of domestic duties (Friedan, 1963; Karpf, 1987). Nevertheless, I maintain that reclamation of the home as a space for girls' technological engagement still affords an active positioning that accords a high degree of agency to the girls involved. For this small group of female pupils, reclaiming the domestic setting as a positive and empowering environment in which to compose had significant benefits. Laura had the music software 'Cakewalk' on her home computer and said she used it for about two hours per week. However, when I asked her how many hours she used music technology at school she said none:

> Laura: I've got a computer at home with music stuff.
> VA: And how much do you use that?
> Laura: I use that mainly for composition and stuff and a bit on harmony.
> VA: And what about the stuff at school?
> Laura: I don't use it very much because there aren't any to use.
> VA: What, even after school?
> Laura: Well, it's easier to go home.
> VA: But you haven't got Cubase at home have you?
> Laura: No, not the same one but I can use what I've got.
> VA: When you encounter technical problems how do you solve them?

Laura: Look up the help bit and stuff and read what it says. You sort of go away for a bit and then come back later and it usually sorts itself out. It's just a slow process of trial and error.

VA: Do you feel more confident now that you've got it at home?

Laura: Yeah. It's easier now. (A level girl, New Tech Comprehensive)

Despite her reservations about the boundaries the home constructs for female musicians, Citron maintains that we can see the home, as a female domain, as representing 'an important site of feminine culture' which could function as 'a meaningful sign of creative authority' (1993: 106). She cites the accomplished musician Fanny Hensel as one such example. Although unable to take up a professional career as a composer, she was able to exert significant power and influence over the acclaimed musical gatherings that took place in her family home. It could not afford her the type of public, professional acclaim experienced by her brother, Felix Mendelssohn, but it did offer her an important musical outlet over which she had considerable control (Citron, 1993: 106; Reich, 1993: 140–42).

Conclusion

Determinist discourses fail to account for the social context in which learning takes place, both the classroom and the computer being socially constructed spaces in which gendered social relations are played out. The emergence of the home as an important theme in the accounts of female pupils and their technological interactions when composing was not expected, although perhaps it is not that surprising given the growing attention researchers are paying to children's home computer use. This chapter offers a glimpse into the ways in which girls take an active approach to working with technology in a safe environment where problems are solved in their own time and in their own ways, although it is important to note that this is not the case for *all* girls as some found the technology itself a barrier to composing, which was discussed in Chapter 6. Despite instances of girls engaging with music technology at home, their numbers and level of use were still comparatively small to that of boys in the study. For example, when asked how much time they spent using compositional software at home, responses ranged from one boy's assertion that he spent around six to ten hours a week using technology at home to another girl's response of 'about ten minutes a month!' However, those girls who did show an interest in using music technology were more likely to engage with it at home than at school, even if it was for short periods. Significantly, these included some of the same girls who expressed the highest levels of technological confidence discussed in Chapter 3.

Within the classroom, girls can find it difficult to actively participate in the construction of them as technological even if they wish to do so, resulting in teachers' perceptions of them as 'traditional' and non-technological. To counteract this, I suggested that the reclaiming of the traditionally feminine/private space of the home in which to work with music technologies might provide an environment that circumvents the powerful masculine–technology relations produced in the classroom. This allowed these young composers to negotiate an identity that incorporated technological know-how and gave them ownership of their skills (Henwood et al., 2000). Admittedly, these subjective experiences may not be able to influence the dominant gendered constructions of the classroom, but there is a sense that some degree of power and control is being grasped by these young female composers, and should be acknowledged as an important aspect of girls' engagement with music technologies.

Chapter 8
Conclusion

The motivation for this book was a response to what I perceived as an increasingly determinist turn in recent discussions about technology in music education. Current debates tend to focus on pedagogical issues and educational outcomes that uncritically construct technology as little more than a 'tool' for composition, rarely acknowledging the sociocultural context of its use and the socially constructed nature of computers. The orthodoxy of technological determinism remains enormously powerful in constructing common-sense assumptions about children and digital technologies as evidenced by Government education policy directives, so it is evident that these assumptions are not confined to the music classroom. Rather problematically, these technocratic discourses are in danger of producing an 'ideal' child user, one who is perceived as confident and eager to engage with all forms of technology. Unfortunately, this invokes a 'natural' affinity between children and technology that rarely goes unchallenged, and these discourses are certainly in evidence in the music classroom. Moreover, this also contributes to the production of determinist discourses that focus too narrowly on what are invariably presented as the positive 'impacts' of music technology by which technology is able to effect change and improvement and in which digital spaces are conceptualized as potentially empowering and democratizing.

However, as I demonstrated in Chapter 1, this partial view renders the social aspects of technology invisible, which I suggested was problematic because of the similar ways in which both technology and music composition have been socially and historically associated with men and masculinity. As Selwyn (2008) notes, there is an urgent need for a more theoretically sophisticated understanding of the relationship between young people and new technologies in particular contexts. To this end, I have taken the view throughout this book that technology is socially embedded and forms part of a relationship creating complex connections with other social relations and institutions (Williams, 1981). Drawing explicitly on perspectives from the sociology of science and technology studies (STS), my theoretical position has been informed by the work of Mackenzie and Wajcman (1999), which views technology and society as mutually constitutive, and which provides a more nuanced perspective that does not view technology as having a unidirectional 'impact' on society. Feminist STS has shown the many ways in which technologies become gendered in wider society; it is probable that taking a digitally mediated approach to music composition will reproduce and reinforce existing gendered social relations rather than affording opportunities to challenge or reconfigure social relations in educational spaces. If, as feminist STS has shown, men have more power to decide what counts as technology this has important implications for the music classroom. Why should a computer, itself socially constructed, be able to reconfigure gendered social relations if, as Turkle (1984) argues, they are constructed as male domains? May (2002: 2) rightly asserts that 'when we strip away the shiny new products and services which are available to us in ever increasing quantities, much about the world has not changed', and it is incumbent upon music educators to acknowledge that gender is 'as an integral part of the social shaping of technology' (Faulkner, 2001: 90). This is an important observation and one that requires serious consideration when critically exploring the processes and practices by which technologies become gendered in the music technology classroom.

My findings show that male teachers and male pupils more frequently engage in technological talk and interactions in ways that marginalize and exclude female teachers and female pupils, processes and practices that contribute to the gendering of technology as masculine. I went on to show how boys and male teachers were constructed as the technological experts, and I argued that this was linked to issues of control, mastery and skill, aspects of hegemonic masculine identity (Connell, 1995) that were particularly prized at New Tech Comprehensive, Old Tech Grammar and to a slightly lesser degree at Arts College. Even Crossways Independent, despite not being implicated in an overtly gendered technological discourse, participated in a strongly gendered musical discourse that privileged a certain type of compositional identity, an identity grounded within the normative expectations of the male 'genius' composer (Battersby, 1989) that gave greater autonomy, physical and creative freedom to the male students. Furthermore, as girls expressed far lower levels of confidence in their technological abilities (findings which support and affirm the conclusions of other researchers particularly in co-educational settings), this may produce a situation in which males are better able to control meanings about what counts and who counts in this environment, and it is often difficult for females to be accorded expert status with regard to both composition and technology irrespective of whether or not they have this expertise. This in turn contributes to the perception that female teachers and pupils are both less interested in technology and less capable of working with it. To counter this, by revealing the gendered discourses in operation in the classroom I suggest that it is not the case that girls lack either interest or ability, but that their apparent 'alienation' and circumspection about digitally mediated composition lies in the ways in which technology continues to be culturally constructed as masculine within the classroom. I have viewed the classroom as an established culture in which teachers and pupils share expectations about the setting: what is valued, taught and learned and how this is socially organized (Sheingold et al., 1984); therefore, it is not technology itself that is the 'problem' for women but the cultural context in which it is used.

Implications for practice

While future governments will undoubtedly continue to tinker with the curriculum, one thing is for certain: the role of technology will not diminish, and the determinist rhetoric currently in evidence is unlikely to disappear as a driver for educational change. Therefore, the remainder of this chapter offers some suggestions for future educational practice in which music classrooms will undoubtedly become more rather than less technologized. At this juncture I am at pains to point out that I am not presenting these suggestions as a series of 'tips for teachers'. I fully recognize that this would oversimplify the complex gendered nature of classroom cultures and how these are produced, and I am well aware that asking teachers to implement a few simple strategies is unlikely to fully address the gender issues I have highlighted in this book. In fact, as I have continually argued, because it is the culture of the classroom that needs to be placed under scrutiny, in order for real change to take place we must recognize that this will take time and resolve on the part of teachers, teacher trainers and even pupils. Those involved in teaching in music departments that use technology, whether within primary, secondary or higher education, must be encouraged to work together to develop meaningful discussions that move beyond simplistic notions of technology as a tool for composition in ways that allow for a more socially embedded and critical understanding of how gender–technology relations are constructed in educational spaces.

I therefore offer the following more in the spirit of some small, but hopefully helpful steps on the way to achieving greater educational inclusion. Of course, this will take time. At a recent European Association for the Study of Science and Technology (EASST) I attended, one conference delegate attending a session on gender and technology noted rather gloomily at the end that 'We have been doing this type of research for *years* now but nothing seems to change'. Similarly, gender research in education has been on the agenda since the 1980s and, while gains have been made and a far greater understanding of gender issues is now available, we are not there yet when it comes to gender equality. However, while I sympathize with the delegate's frustration, there is much to take heart from, and the following is offered in the spirit of continued endeavour and enquiry. As I pointed out in Chapter 1, despite determinist rhetoric, those working in technologized music spaces do have agency and can shape new ways of thinking about composition in digitally mediated spaces that will allow for all pupils to develop an affirmatory composition identity that involves them making choices about their mode of composition and what they wish to write, and ensuring that all their contributions, whether technological or non-technological, are equally valued.

Teacher training and continuing professional development

To seriously challenge the masculinist technocratic discourses in operation requires more than a neat set of tools that, if dutifully followed, will transform teaching spaces so that gender will no longer require critical attention. What has become apparent in recent times is that teaching about gender on teacher-training courses receives minimal attention. It therefore seems reasonable to suggest that this is likely to have a negative effect on the classroom because, while trainees may have some understanding of gender issues in relation to pedagogic practice, as Younger (2007) observes, these can lead to oversimplified and often essentialized perceptions of the educational needs of boys and girls, such as boys being more motivated by competitive styles of working. His findings show that only 13 per cent of trainees surveyed thought that girls experienced any form of educational disadvantage in school. In a recent survey of newly qualified primary teachers carried out by the Training and Development Agency (TDA), teachers were asked to comment on the extent to which their training had equipped them to work with pupils from ethnic minority backgrounds, those with special educational needs and pupils who had English as an additional language, but the survey did not require information regarding trainees' understanding of gender issues (Younger and Warrington, 2008). Given that gender issues have become increasingly focused on boys' underachievement and the need for curricula and pedagogy to be more amendable to boys' interests, this is rather worrying leading Younger and Warrington (2008) to assert that, while boys' educational needs are being accommodated, there is certainly a sense of 'gender invisibility' that fails to address the educational needs and experiences of girls in current teacher-training content.

Therefore, to only address pedagogic issues when discussing gender is likely to mean that teachers will not develop a real understanding of the crucial role they play in constructing gendered discourses in their classrooms because they do not have the requisite theoretical tools at their disposal. Firstly, what is required is a heightened awareness that gender must remain firmly on the agenda as an issue for the music classroom. Green's (1997) work in this area was a crucial text in helping to understand the gendered nature of the music classroom, and offered important insights into the gendering of composition, but technology warranted limited discussion at the time. In the intervening years since her book was published, the burgeoning of technology as a medium for composition in the compulsory school classroom has been significant, and we have also seen enormous growth in the number of undergraduate and postgraduate music technology courses now being offered at university. It therefore seems timely that teacher training for music teachers and continuing professional development for more experienced educators should pay greater critical attention to how gendered social relations are constructed in technological spaces and the educator's role within this construction.

The problems of single-sex classes

My findings suggest that the ways girls approach learning about technology is slightly different from the approach taken by boys, and often reflects their out-of-school digital activities and interests. In line with other research, girls in my study said that they would appreciate more structured help and training with new music software but I have some reservations about advocating that this take place in single-sex settings as some researchers have advocated (Colley et al., 1997). As Culley (1988) has noted, in taking such an approach, there may be a tendency to 'ghettoize' girls-only sessions, particularly when taught by staff not perceived as particularly technologically proficient, and this clearly has serious implications for classroom practice. While Culley acknowledged that girls may be less inclined to use computer rooms where boys dominate (and this was certainly the case at Crossways Independent and New Tech Comprehensive), girls-only schemes may serve to further diminish girls' access because the 'open' sessions continue to be dominated by boys. I am concerned that, by providing separate sessions for girls, there is a serious risk of producing a subordinate female subculture in which 'female technology' might be unfairly compared to 'male technology'. This concern is reinforced by the observation I made that a significant number of the girls within my study stated that they had not been given the same training in certain types of software as the boys in their class, resulting in fewer girls expressing the confidence or having sufficient knowledge to use the more complex and highly valued sequencing packages in their work. My findings suggest that the meanings around music software are also highly gendered, therefore certain types of software may be more compatible with and reflect gendered assumptions about the user. The more complicated the software the more likely it was to be associated with a male expert user in contrast to simpler notational software which boys (and some girls) were less likely to associate with 'real' music technology. Boys in my study are expected to be secure in their identity as computer users, which in part is associated with the ability to use more complex music software and its association with masculine characteristics of skill and expertise. Therefore it was a worrying observation that boys were often the recipients of more 'complex' technological information whereby teachers tended to introduce boys to advanced sequencing software on an 'ad hoc' informal basis. There were certainly boys within my study who were not proficient technology users but they were less likely or less willing to express any sense of 'lack'. Therefore, by offering more structured approaches to learning about music software so that extra support can be provided to both male and female pupils, all pupils will have access to the same degree of technological information that may help to reduce this inequality of access to different types of music software. In addition, it may also lead teachers to re-examine their perceptions about 'male expertise' that presupposes that all boys are more interested and capable users of technology, and to provide girls with the same opportunities to demonstrate expertise on more sophisticated software.

Greater awareness about how male and female teachers and pupils are differently positioned in the technologized classroom

Throughout this study, I have emphasized the central role played by the teacher in constructing gendered technological discourses. I have argued that men's symbolic association with technology is an important aspect in constructions of masculinity, and my study demonstrates that male teachers and pupils positively align themselves with all things technological. This affords them greater control to name what counts and who counts in technological spaces, and who can be constructed as the technological expert. Game and Pringle (1984) state that men have more power to say what they will and will not do, and consequently have a greater influence over the cultural and material practices within the workplace. Men's experiences feed into pre-existing masculine cultures from which women are already excluded. In addition to these formal male networks are those informal networks around which 'masculine' cultures develop. Few women either wish to or are able to participate in them and are thereby left out of an important part of the loop. As Lamb (1993: 175) observes, 'it becomes apparent that men, as a class, define the structures of power and maintain the relations of ruling within music and music education'. This in turn impacts negatively on pupils' perceptions of female teachers. Female teachers are considered less interested and less able to engage with music composition technologies. Where they do so, their engagement is perceived as requiring very little skill or technical expertise, such as printing off parts for rehearsals. This contributes to the ways in which male teachers and male pupils work together to produced gendered discourses to which female teachers and female pupils find themselves unable to contribute. Pupils' perceptions will be significantly influenced by the gender of the teacher to act as a role-model (Green, 1997). It is therefore important for teachers to begin to develop self-awareness as to how their social interactions around technology are perceived. As I demonstrated in my discussion of the construction of the pupil expert, female teachers can often undermine not only their own authority and identity but also that of their female pupils when they insist on privileging boys' technical knowledge over that of girls. Male teachers should attempt to encourage girls to participate in technological discussions that are more often than not monopolized by boys. This would send out a clear message that girls' knowledge is equally valued, and their technological interactions will be more overtly recognized.

Using older girls to mentor younger girls and boys may also reduce the masculine connotations of computers and music software. If girls are seen to talk about and use technology knowledgeably and confidently, the symbolic associations of technology with masculinity could perhaps be minimized. Female role models are important to other women, as the following comment by a female audio production postgraduate student illustrates:

> The few female teachers that I have encountered during my four years in music/technology education have been tremendous role models for me. I don't think they were trying to be role models. It is often enough that they are there. (Whistlecroft, 2000: 5)

By encouraging more confident technological girls to work with less confident girls during composition lessons, their knowledge, and indeed their very presence in the music technology suite, may serve to alter negative perceptions about girls' technological competence.

Providing greater flexibility in the compositional process

Throughout the book I have attempted to show why it is important that pupils have some level of control over their digital and non-digital interactions in their compositional processes. It is vital that teachers, wherever possible, do not equate 'composition' with 'music technology suite'. It has been highlighted that such a strongly circumscribed approach to the use of technology poses particular challenges for girls but it is certainly not unproblematic for some boys too although, as my findings suggest, they appear to have access to a wider range of acceptable forms of masculinity (such as the 'rock' musician) that were not available to the girls. If other modes of composition are available, students should be offered the opportunity to use these rather than compel all students to compose in the same way.

While Haraway's cyborg as a concept for feminist analysis continues to stimulate our imaginations, I have suggested that as a political image it has been less successful. As Squires notes, persuasive rhetoric alone will not be sufficient to alter the distribution of power. Like many feminists, she does not deny the usefulness of the cyborg image but feels that it has been 'submerged beneath a sea of technophoric cyberdrool' (2000: 360). She rightly asserts that the image of the cyborg can only be salvaged if it is seen 'as a metaphor for addressing the interrelation between technology and the body, not as a means of using the former to transcend the latter' (2000: 360). This observation highlights the tensions between cyberfeminists who have seized on the cyborg as the ontological future and those feminists, and here I include myself, who wish to see the body included in discussions about technology. Without this sense of the corporeal, we are in danger of losing the political plot. Whatever the acts of 'cyborgian' engagement envisioned by Haraway, these are all initiated from the corporeal, and it is this that grounds us in real, lived, social relations. The idea that the materiality of our existence could or should be extinguished seems to be a frantic attempt to align us with technology, as if our 'cyborgian' selves were entirely transcendent of material concerns. Rather worryingly, it further suggests that the corporeal (and here I am referring to both men's and women's bodies) can be re-drawn *at will* via a new technological embodiment which transcends (or ignores) cultural markers or by attempting to obliterate the body completely. Neither of these formulations appears satisfactory because notions of identity become completely divorced from our real, lived, social relations. I therefore maintain that we must focus on the *materiality* of human–machine amalgams and focus on the degree of choice and level of agency afforded to these young composers in my study.

Conclusion

My contention is that boys and girls have agency to choose what subject positions they adopt, but I have argued that this is within a particular cultural and structural context. Therefore, the degree to which this is possible is circumscribed by the classroom cultures in which they operate. It would appear, from my findings, that although girls do find spaces to develop a technological and compositional identity, this is made particularly difficult in cultures that produce an overtly technological discourse in which girls and women are rendered invisible, and opportunities to exhibit highly valued compositional and technological skills – more commonly associated with masculinity – are hard to come by. While it is apparent that compositional music technology has significant practical benefits for many, my findings highlight that we must not lose sight of the sociocultural aspects of computers and their use in which gender–technology relations are constituted. Despite arguments for technology's 'democratizing' potential, it appears that there are gender differences, not in any innate, essentializing way, but differences produced through the reproduction of gendered understandings of technology within society. These differences are produced through discourses that posit boys and male teachers as the technological experts, and where boys are given greater compositional autonomy in contexts in which boys' musical deviance will not only be tolerated but contribute to teachers' perceptions of male pupils as confident and competent technologists and composers.

The relationship between gender and music technology should remain an important empirical question for music educators when thinking about compositional practices mediated via technology. If girls are also to have positive experiences of composition and technology, music educators must be mindful of difference and plurality. Gender equity within the technologized music classroom goes far beyond issues of equal access. It comes through an awareness of how language, behaviour, values, organizational issues, texts, music software and knowledge all contribute to the shaping of gendered meanings that enter into our classroom practices and reproduce normative gendered expectations. This is especially pertinent given that music technology is becoming increasingly central to music-making practices in educational settings across all sectors of education from primary to higher education. It is essential that we recognize what composition (which extends far beyond the narrow parameters of the curriculum) *means* to these young composers. Composition serves as an important medium for the affirmation of self and identity, and we would do well to remember this in our uncritical embracing of technology if we hope to achieve a truly inclusive music classroom that values the contributions and talents of all its pupils. I will end the book with a short extract from my conversation with Carolyn, an enthusiastic, curious young composer whose poignant words so eloquently summarize so many of the themes I have explored:

Carolyn: I love composing when I'm allowed to sit down and write completely what I want but when you've got to think 'oh, it's got to have this technique' or make sure that you're showing you can do 'this' and it's got to be done by such and such a time, you kind of get bogged down in the kind of mathematics of it instead of the creative side and I think that's a bit of shame, because that's the part I enjoy.

VA: So how did you feel about the compositions you've written? Are they less satisfying when you are given a stimulus?

Carolyn: I wouldn't say less satisfying because you're always sort of proud of yourself when you come away with a composition that sounds good ... you can say 'I've done that' ... there's not much emotional attachment to the piece. I suppose that's a bit of a shame because that's what music is about for me. (A level girl, Crossways Independent)

Bibliography

Abbis, J. (2008). 'Rethinking the "problem" of gender and IT schooling: discourses in literature', *Gender and Education*, 20(2), pp 153–65.

Acker, S. (1994). *Gendered education*, Open University Press.

Adam, A. (1998). *Artificial knowing: gender and the thinking machine*, Routledge.

Adorno, T. (1928). 'The curves of the needle', *Musikblatter des Anbruch*, 10, pp 47–50; trans. Thomas Y. Levin, *October 55* (Winter 1990), pp 48–55.

Airy, S. and Parr, J.M. (2001). 'MIDI, music and me: students' perspectives on composing with MIDI', *Music Education Research*, 3(2), pp 41–9.

Alemany Gomez, M. (1994). 'Bodies, machines and male power' in C. Cockburn and R. Furst-Dilic (eds) *Bringing technology home*, Open University Press.

Allard, A.C. (2004). 'Speaking of gender: teachers' metaphorical constructs of male and female students', *Gender and Education*, 16(3), pp 347–63.

Alldred, P. (1998). 'Ethnography and discourse analysis: dilemmas in representing the voices of children' in J. Ribbens and R. Edwards (eds) *Feminist dilemmas in qualitative research*, Sage Publications.

AQA (2008). *General certificate of education, music: report on the examination* http://store.aqa.org.uk/qual/pdf/AQA-3271A-WRE-JUN08.PDF (last accessed 2 June 2011).

Archer, L. and Francis, B. (2006). *Understanding minority ethnic achievement: race, gender, class and 'success'*, Routledge.

Armstrong, V. (1999). *Styles of mastery: gender, composition and technology*, unpublished MA dissertation, University of London, Institute of Education.

Armstrong, V. (2001). 'Theorizing gender and music composition in the computerized classroom', *Women: A Cultural Review*, 12(1), pp 35–43.

Armstrong, V. (2008). 'Hard bargaining on the hard drive: gender bias in the music technology classroom', *Gender and Education*, 20(4), pp 375–86.

Arnot, M. (2002). *Reproducing gender: essays on educational theory and feminist politics*, RoutledgeFalmer.

Arnot, M. and Weiner, G. (eds) (1987). *Gender under scrutiny: new inquiries in education*, Falmer.

Askew, S. and Ross, C. (1988). *Boys don't cry: boys and sexism in education*. Open University Press.

Baldock, K. (2009). '"Girls and boys come out to play": my journey in gender and education' in S.D. Harrison (ed.) *Male voices: stories of boys learning through music*, ACER Press.

Balsamo, A. (1999). 'Reading cyborgs writing feminism' in J. Wolmark (ed.) *Cybersexualities: a reader on feminist theory, cyborgs and cyberspace*, Edinburgh University Press.

Barker, C. (2000). *Cultural studies: theory and practice*, Sage Publications.

Barthes, R. (1977). *Image-Music-Text*. Fontana.

Battersby, C. (1989). *Gender and genius: towards a feminist aesthetics*, The Women's Press.

Battersby, C. (1999). 'Her bodies/her boundaries' in J. Price and M. Shildrick (eds) *Feminist theory and the body: a reader*, Edinburgh University Press.

Bayton, M. (1997). 'Women and the electric guitar', in S. Whiteley (ed.), *Sexing the groove*, Routledge.

Bayton, M. (1998). *Frock rock: women performing popular music*, Oxford University Press.

BECTA (2002). *ImpaCT2 – the impact of information and communication technologies on pupil learning and attainment*, report, British Educational Communications and Technology Agency, www.becta.org.uk/research/impaCT2 [last accessed 30 October 2010].

BECTA (2007). *Evaluation of the ICT test bed project*, report, British Educational Communications and Technology Agency, www.evaluation.icttestbed.org.uk/files/test_bed_evaluation_2006_learning.pdf [last accessed 31 October 2010].

BECTA (2008). *How do boys and girls differ in their use of ICT?*, report, British Educational Communications and Technology Agency.

BECTA (2009). *Harnessing technology – emerging technology trends*, report, British Educational Communications and Technology Agency.

Berg, A.J. (1994). 'Technological flexibility: bringing gender into technology' in C. Cockburn and R. Furst-Dilic (eds) *Bringing technology home*, Open University Press.

Beyer, K.W. (2009). *Grace Hopper and the innovation of the information age*, MIT Press.

Bijker, W.E., Hughes, T.P. and Pinch, T.J. (eds) (1990). *The social construction of technological systems: new directions in the sociology of history and technology* (3rd edition), MIT Press.

Boehm, C. (2007). 'The discipline that never was: current developments in music technology in higher education in Britain', *Journal of Music, Technology and Education*, 1(1), pp 7–21.

Bowers, J. and Tick, J. (eds) (1986). *Women making music: the Western art tradition, 1150–1950*, University of Illinois Press.

Bradby, B. (1993). 'Sampling sexuality: gender, technology and the body', *Popular Music*, 12(2), pp 155–76.

Bromley, H. (1997). 'The social chicken and the technological egg: educational computing and the technology/society divide', *Educational Theory*, 47(1), pp 51–65.

Bromley, H. (1998). 'Introduction: data-driven democracy? Social assessment of educational computing', in H. Bromley and M.W. Apple (eds), *Education/technology/power: educational computing as social practice*, State University of New York Press.

Bromley, H. and Apple, M.W. (eds) (1998). *Education/technology/power: educational computing as social practice*, State University of New York Press.

Buckingham, D. (2007). *Beyond technology: children's learning in the age of digital culture*, Polity Press.

Buckingham, D. and Willett, R. (2006). *Digital generations: children, young people, and the new media*, Routledge.

Bunting, R. (2002). 'The place of composing in the Music curriculum', in G. Spruce (ed.), *Teaching music in secondary schools: a reader*, London: RoutledgeFalmer

Burnard, P. (2007). 'Creativity and technology: critical agents of change in the work and lives of music teachers' in J. Finney and P. Burnard (eds) *Music education with digital technology*, Continuum.

Busen-Smith, M. (1999). 'Developing strategies', *British Journal of Music Education*, 16(2), pp 197–213.

Byrne, C. and MacDonald, R.A.R. (2002). 'The use of information and communication technology (I&CT) in the Scottish music curriculum: a focus group investigation of themes and issues', *Music Education Research*, 4(2), pp 263–73.

Cameron, J. (1984). *The Terminator.* Orion.

Caputo, V. (1994). 'Add technology and stir', *Quarterly Journal of Music Teaching and Learning*, 4(4)–5(1), pp 85–90.

Chandra, V. and Lloyd, M. (2008). 'The methodological nettle: ICT and student achievement', *British Journal of Educational Technology*, 39(6), pp 1087–98.

Cherny, W. and Reba Weise, E. (eds) (1996). *Wired women: gender and new realities and cyberspace*, Seal Press.

Citron, M. (1993). *Gender and the musical canon*, Cambridge University Press.

Clarricoates, K. (1978). 'Dinosaurs in the classroom – a re-examination of some aspects of the "hidden curriculum" in primary schools', *Women's Studies International Quarterly*, 1, pp 353–64.

Clegg, S. (2001). 'Theorising the machine: gender, education and computing', *Gender and Education*, 13(3), pp 307–24.

Cockburn, C. (1985). *Machinery of dominance: women, men and technical know-how.* Pluto.

Cockburn, C. (1999a). 'Caught in the wheels: the high cost of being a female cog in the male machinery of engineering' in D. Mackenzie and J. Wajcman (eds) *The social shaping of technology*, Open University Press.

Cockburn, C. (1999b). 'The material of male power' in D. Mackenzie and J. Wajcman (eds) *The social shaping of technology*, Open University Press.

Cockburn, C. and Furst-Dilic, R. (eds) (1994). *Bringing technology home*, Open University Press.

Coffey, A. and Delamont, S. (2000). *Feminism and the classroom teacher: research, practice and pedagogy*, RoutledgeFalmer.

Cohen, S. (1991). *Rock culture in Liverpool*, Oxford University Press.

Colley, A. and Comber, C. (2003). 'Age and gender differences in computer use and attitudes among secondary school students: what has changed?' *Educational Research*, 45(2), pp 155–65.

Colley, A., Comber, C. and Hargreaves, J. (1997). 'IT and music education: what happens to boys and girls in co-educational and single sex schools?' *British Journal of Music Education*, 14(2), pp 119–27.

Comber, C., Hargreaves, D.J. and Colley A. (1993), 'Girls, boys and technology in music education', *British Journal of Music Education*, 10, pp 123–34.

Connell, R.W. (1995), *Masculinities*, Polity Press.

Cook, S.C. and Tsou, J.S. (1994). *Cecilia reclaimed: feminist perspectives on gender and music*. University of Illinois Press.

Cooper, J. (2006). 'The digital divide: the special case of gender', *Journal of Computer Assisted Learning*, 22, pp 320–34.

Cooper, L. (2007). 'The gender factor: teaching composition in music technology lessons to boys and girls in Year 9', in J. Finney and P. Burnard (eds), *Music education with digital technology*, Continuum.

Cranmer, S., Potter, J. and Selwyn, N. (2008). *Learners and technology: 7–11*, report, British Educational Communications and Technology Agency.

Culley, L. (1988). 'Girls, boys and computers', *Educational Studies*, 14(1), pp 3–8.

Cunningham, H. (1998). 'Digital culture: a view from the dance floor' in J. Sefton-Green (ed.) *Digital diversions: youth culture in the age of multimedia*, UCL Press.

Davis, K. (1997). 'Embody-ing theory: beyond modernist and postmodernist readings of the body' in K. Davis (ed.) *Embodied practices: feminist perspectives on the body*, Sage Publications.

Denzin, N. and Lincoln, Y. (1998). *Collecting and interpreting qualitative materials*, Sage Publications.

DfES (2003). 'Fulfilling the potential: transforming teaching and learning through ICT in schools', http://publications.teachernet.gov.uk [last accessed 12 March 2004].

Dibben, N. (2002). 'Gender identity and music', in R.A.R Macdonald, D.J. Hargreaves and D. Miell (eds) *Musical identities*, Oxford University Press.

Dickinson, K. (2001). '"Believe"? Vocoders, digitalised female identity and camp', *Popular Music*, 20(3), pp 333–47.

Dillabough, J. (2001). 'Gender theory and research in education: modernist traditions and emerging contemporary themes' in B. Francis and C. Skelton (eds) *Investigating gender: contemporary perspectives in education*, Open University Press.

Dunn, L. and Jones, N.A. (eds) (1994). *Embodied voices: representing female vocality in western culture*, Cambridge University Press.

Epstein, D. and Johnson, R. (1998). *Schooling sexualities*, Open University Press.

Epstein, D., Elwood, J., Hey, V. and Maw, J. (eds) (1998). *Failing boys? Issues in gender and achievement*, Open University Press.

Facer, K., Furlong, J., Furlong, R. and Sutherland, R. (2001). 'Home is where the hardware is: young people, the domestic environment and "access" to new technologies' in I. Hutchby and J. Moran-Ellis (eds) *Children, technology and culture: the impacts of technologies in children's everyday lives*, RoutledgeFalmer.

Facer, K., Furlong J., Furlong, R. and Sutherland, R. (2003). *Screen play: children and computing at home* RoutledgeFalmer.

Farrar, V. (2007). *Diversity within the International Centre for Music at Newcastle University: a quantitative study*, Centre for Excellence in Teaching and Learning.

Faulkner, W. (2001). 'The technology question in feminism: a view from feminist technology studies', *Women's Studies International Forum*, 4(2), pp 79–95.

Faulkner, W. and Arnold, E. (eds) (1985). *Smothered by invention: technology in women's lives*, Pluto Press.

Feldberg, R.L. and Glenn, E.N. (1983) 'Technology and work degradations: effects of office automation on women clerical workers' in J. Rothschild (ed.) *Machina ex dea: feminist perspectives on technology*, Pergamon.

Ferrero, S. (2007). 'A "bounded virtuality": ICTs and youth in Alghero, Sardinia', in P. Hodkinson and W. Deicke (eds), *Youth cultures: scenes, subcultures and tribes*, Routledge.

Folkestad, G. (1998). 'Musical learning as cultural practice: as exemplified in computer-based creative music-making' in B. Sundin, G. McPherson and G. Folkestad (eds) *Children composing*, Lund University Press.

Folkestad, G., Hargreaves, D.J. and Lindstrom, B. (1998). 'A typology of composition styles', *British Journal of Music Education*, 15(1), pp 83–97.

Francis, B. (2000). *Boys, girls and achievement: addressing the classroom issues'*, Routledge Falmer.

Francis, B. (2001). 'Beyond postmodernism: feminist agency in educational research' in B. Francis and C. Skelton (eds) *Investigating gender: contemporary perspectives in education*, Open University Press.

Francis, B. and Skelton, C. (eds) (2001). *Investigating gender: contemporary perspectives in education*, Open University Press.

Freedman, D. (2003). 'Raymond Williams', in C. May (ed.) *Key thinkers for the information society*, Routledge.

Friedan, B. (1963). *The feminine mystique*, Penguin Books.

Frith, S. (1996). *Performing rites: evaluating popular music*, Oxford University Press.

Frith, S. and McRobbie, A. (1978/79). 'Rock and sexuality', *Screen Education*, 29, pp 3–19.

Gall, M. and Breeze, N. (2005). 'Music composition lessons: the multimodal affordances of technology', *Educational Review*, 57(4), pp 415–33.

Game, A. and Pringle, R. (1984). *Gender at work.* Pluto Press.

Gilbert, J. and Pearson, E. (1999). *Discographies: dance music, culture and the politics of sound*, Routledge.

Glover, J. (2000). *Children composing 4–14*, RoutledgeFalmer.

Gonçalves, F. (2004). 'Performing the Trojan horse: Laurie Anderson's strategies of resistance and the "postmedia era"', *Body, Space and Technology Journal*, 2(2), http://people.brunel.ac.uk/bst/vol0202/index.html (last accessed 3 June 2011).

Gonzalez, J. (2000). 'Envisioning cyborg bodies: notes from current research' in G. Kirkup, L. Janes, K. Woodward and F. Hovenden (eds) *The gendered cyborg: a reader*, Routledge.

Green, L. (1997). *Music, gender and education*, Cambridge University Press.

Green, L. (2002). *How popular musicians learn: a way ahead for music education*, Ashgate Publishing.

Green, L. (2003). 'Why "ideology" is still relevant for critical thinking in music education', *Action, Criticism and Theory for Music Education*, 2(2), www.siue.educ/MUSIC/ACTPAPERS/v2/Green03.pdf [last accessed 28 January 2004].

Green, L. (2008). *Music, informal learning and the school: a new classroom pedagogy*, Ashgate Publishing.

Green, E. and Adam, A. (eds) (2001). *Virtual gender: technology, consumption and identity*, Routledge.

Green, E., Owen, J. and Pain, D. (eds) (1993). *Gendered by design: information technology and office systems*, Taylor & Francis.

Griffiths, P. (1985). *New sounds, new personalities: British composers of the 1980s in conversation with Paul Griffiths*, Faber Music.

Grint, K. and Gill, R. (eds) (1995). *The gender–technology relation: contemporary theory and research*, Taylor & Francis.

Grint, K. and Woolgar, S. (1995). 'On some failures of nerve in constructivist and feminist analyses of technology' in K. Grint and R. Gill (eds) *The gender–technology relation*, Taylor & Francis.

Grosz, E. (1994). *Volatile bodies: toward a corporeal feminism*, Indiana University Press.

Haddon, L. and Skinner, D. (1991). 'The enigma of the micro: lessons from the British home computer boom', *Social Science Computer Review*, 9, pp 435–51

Halstead, J. (1997). *The woman composer: creativity and the gendered politics of musical composition*, Ashgate Publishing.

Hammersley, M. and Atkinson, P. (1983). *Ethnography: principles in practice*, Routledge.

Hapnes, T. and Sorensen, K.H. (1995). 'Competition and collaboration in male shaping of computing: a study of a Norwegian hacker culture' in K. Grint and R. Gill (eds) *The gender–technology relation: contemporary theory and research*, Taylor & Francis.

Haraway, D. (1990). 'A manifesto for cyborgs: science, technology and socialist feminism in the 1980s' in L. Nicholson *Feminism/postmodernism*, Routledge (first published in *Socialist Review*, 80, 1985).

Harding, S. (1986). *The science question in feminism*, Open University Press.

Harding, S. (1991). *Whose science? Whose knowledge?* Open University Press.

Harrison, S. (2010). 'Boys on the outer: themes in male engagement with music', *Journal of Boyhood Studies*, 4(1), pp 39–53.

Hatfield, J. (2000). 'Disappearing digitally: gender in the digital domain' in Cutting Edge: The Women's Research Group *Digital desires: language, identity and new technologies*, I.B. Tauris.

Haywood, C.P. and Mac an Ghaill, M. (2003). *Men and masculinities*, Open University Press.

Heath, S., Brooks, R., Cleaver, E. and Ireland, E. (2009). *Researching young people's lives*, Sage Publications.

Heemskerk, I., ten Dam, G., Volman, M. and Admiraal, W. (2009). 'Gender inclusiveness in educational technology and learning experiences of girls and boys', *Journal of Research on Technology in Education*, 41(3), pp 253–76.

Henwood, F. (1993). 'Establishing gender perspectives on information technology' in E. Green, J. Owen, J. and D. Pain (eds), *Gendered by design: information technology and office systems*, Taylor & Francis.

Henwood, F., Plumeridge, S. and Stepulevage, L. (2000). 'A tale of two cultures? Gender and inequality in computer education', in S. Wyatt, F. Henwood, N. Miller and P. Senker (eds), *Technology and in/equality: questioning the information society*, Routledge.

Henwood, F., Wyatt, S., Miller, N. and Senker, P. (2000). 'Critical perspectives on technologies, in/equalities and the information society', in S. Wyatt, F. Henwood, N. Miller and P. Senker (eds), *Technology and in/equality: questioning the information society*, Routledge.

Hew, K.F. (2009). 'Use of audio podcast in K-12 and higher education: a review of research topics and methodologies', *Education Technologies Research and Development*, 57, pp 333–57.

Hickey, M. (1997). 'The computer as a tool in creative music making', *Research Studies in Music Education*, 8, pp 56–70.

Hinkle-Turner, E., Roberts, M.L., Scaletti, C., Rubin, A., Rudow, V.A., Parenti, S., Helmuth, M. and Schieve, C. (1999). 'Forum: composing women' in E. Barkin and L. Hamessley (eds) *Audible traces: gender, identity and music*, Carciofoli Verlagshaus.

Ho, W.C. (2004). 'Attitudes towards information technology in music learning amongst Hong Kong Chinese boys and girls', *British Journal of Music Education*, 21(2), pp 143–61.

Hodges, R. (1996). 'The new technology' in C. Plummeridge (ed.) *Music education: trends and issues*, University of London, Institute of Education.

Hodges, R. (2001). 'Using ICT in music teaching' in C. Philpott and C. Plummeridge (eds) *Issues in music teaching*, RoutledgeFalmer.

Hodges, R. (2007). 'Music education and training: ICT, innovation and curriculum reform' in J. Finney and P. Burnard (eds) *Music education with digital technology*, Continuum.

Holloway, S.L. and Valentine. G. (2003). *Cyberkids: children in the information age*, RoutledgeFalmer.

Huber, B.R. and Schofield, J. (1998), 'I like computers, but many girls don't: gender and sociocultural context of computing' in A. Bromley and M.W. Apple (eds) *Education/technology/power: educational computing as social practice*, State University of New York Press.

Hugill, A. (2008). *The digital musician*, Routledge.

Humm, M. (1995). *The dictionary of feminist theory* (2nd edition) Prentice-Hall/Harvester Wheatsheaf.

Hutchby, I .and Moran-Ellis, J. (2001) (eds), *Children, technology and culture: the impacts of technologies in children's everyday lives'*, RoutledgeFalmer.

Jackson, C. and Dempster, S. (2009). '"I sat back on my computer … with a bottle of whisky next to me": constructing "cool" masculinity through "effortless" achievement in secondary and higher education', *Journal of Gender Studies*, 18(4), pp 341–56.

Jezic, D. (1994). *Women composers: a lost tradition*, Feminist Press.

Jenson, J. and Brushwood-Rose, C. (2003). 'Women@work: listening to gendered relations of power in teachers' talk about new technologies', *Gender and Education*, 15(2), pp 169–82.

Jestrovic, S. (2002). 'The performer and the machine: some aspects of Laurie Anderson's stage work', *Body, Space and Technology*, 1(1), www.brunel.ac.uk/depts/pfa/bstjournal/1no1/SILVIJAJESTROVIC.htm [last accessed 1 September 2002].

Karpf, A. (1987). 'Recent feminist approaches to women and technology' in M. McNeil (ed.) *Gender and expertise*, Free Association Books.

Katz, M. (2004). *Capturing sound: how technology has changed music*, University of California Press.

Kiesler, S., Sproull, L. and Eccles, J.S. (1985). 'Pool halls, chips and war games: women in the culture of computing', *Psychology of Women Quarterly*, 9, pp 451–62.

Kirkup, G., Keller, E. and Smith, L. (1992) (eds). *Inventing women: science, technology and gender*, Polity Press in association with Open University Press.

Kirkup, G., Janes, L., Woodward. K. and Hovenden, F. (eds) (2000). *The gendered cyborg: a reader*, Routledge.

Kramarae, C. (ed.) (1988). *Technology and women's voices*, Routledge and Kegan Paul.

Lamb, R. (1993). 'The possibilities of/for feminist music criticism in music education', *British Journal of Music Education*, 10(3), pp 169–80.

Leitch, S. (2006). *Prosperity for all in the global economy – world class skills: final report*, HM Treasury, www.delni.gov.uk/leitch_finalreport051206[1]-2.pdf (last accessed 3 June 2011).

Lemke, J.C. (1995). *Textual politics: discourse and social dynamics*, Taylor & Francis.

Leonard, M. (2007). *Gender and the music industry: rock, discourse and girl power*, Ashgate Publishing.

LePage, J.W. (1980). *Women composers, conductors, and musicians of the twentieth century: selected biographies*, The Scarecrow Press.

Linn, P. (1987). 'Gender stereotypes, technology stereotypes' in M. McNeil (ed.) *Gender and expertise*, Free Association Books.

Livingstone, S. (2002). *Young people and new media: childhood and the changing media environment*, Sage Publications.

Loader, B.D. (1998). 'Cyberspace divide: equality, agency and policy in the information society' in B.D. Loader (ed.) *Cyberspace divide: equality: agency and policy in the information society*, Routledge.

Loza, S. (2001). 'Sampling (hetero)sexuality: diva-ness and discipline in electronic dance music', *Popular Music*, 20(3), pp 349–57.

Luckin, R., Clark, W., Graber, W., Logan, K., Mee, A. and Oliver, M. (2009). 'Do Web 2.0 tools really open the door to learning? Practices, perceptions and profiles of 11–16 year olds students', *Learning, Media and Technology*, 34(2), pp 87–104.

Mackenzie, D. and Wajcman, J. (eds) (1999). *The social shaping of technology* (2nd edition) Open University Press, first published 1985.

Mansfield, M. (2005). 'The global musical subject, curriculum and Heidegger's questioning concerning technology', *Education Philosophy and Theory*, 37(1), pp 133–48.

May, C. (2002). *The information society: a sceptical view*, Polity Press.

May, C. (ed.) (2003). *Key thinkers for the information society'*, Routledge.

McCartney, A. (1995). 'The ambiguous relation: part 1', *Contact: Journal of the Canadian Electroacoustic Community*, 9(1), pp 43–58, http://cec.concordia.ca/contact/contact9107.html [last accessed 26 October 2010].

McClary, S. (1991). *Feminine endings: music, gender and sexuality*, University of Minneapolis Press.

McGregor, J. (2004). 'Editorial', *FORUM*, 46(1), pp 1–5.

McLuhan, M. (1964). *Understanding media: the extensions of man*, Routledge.

McNeil, M. (ed.) (1987). *Gender and expertise*, Free Association Books.

Mellor, L. (2008). 'Creativity, originality, identity: investigating computer-based composition in secondary schools, *Music Education Research*, 10(4), pp 451–72.

Mills, J. and Murray, A. (2000). 'Music technology inspected: good teaching at Key Stage 3', *British Journal of Music Education*, 17(2), pp 129–56.

Moisala, P. and Diamond, B. (2000) (eds). *Music and Gender*, University of Illinois Press.

Moran-Ellis, J. and Cooper, G. (2000). 'Making connections: children, technology and the National Grid for Learning', *Sociological Research Online*, 5(3), www.socresonline.org.uk/5/3/moran-ellis.html [last accessed 10 October 2002].

Moss, G., Jewitt, C., Levaaic, R., Armstrong, V., Cardini, A. and Castle, F. (2006). *The interactive whiteboards, pedagogy and pupil performance evaluation:*

an evaluation of the schools whiteboard expansion (SWE) project (London Challenge)*, London: DfES. www.dfes.gov.uk/research/data/uploadfiles/ RR816.pdf [last accessed 31 October 2010].

Mumford, L. (1934). *Technics and civilisation*, George Routledge and Sons.

Murphie, A. and Potts, J. (2003). *Culture and technology*, Palgrave Macmillan.

Murray, F. (1993). 'A separate reality: science, technology and masculinity' in E. Green, J. Owen, and D. Pain, (eds) *Gendered by design: information technology and office systems*, Taylor & Francis.

Muso (2005). 'Bending the Rules', April/May, 16, pp 14–19.

Negroponte, N. (1995). *Being Digital*, Coronet/Hodder and Stoughton.

Neuls-Bates, C. (1982). *Women in music: an anthology of source readings from the Middle Ages to the present*, Harper & Row.

Nilsson, B. and Folkestad, G. (2005). 'Children's practice of computer-based composition', *Music Education Research*, 7(1), pp 21–37.

Odam, G. (2002). 'Teaching composing in secondary schools: the creative dream' in G. Spruce (ed.), *Aspects of teaching secondary music: perspectives on practice*, RoutledgeFalmer in association with Open University Press.

Ofsted (2004). *Provision of music services in 15 local education authorities*, Office for Standards in Education.

Ofsted (2009). *Making more of music: an evaluation of music in schools 2005/8*, Office for Standards in Education.

Ormrod, S. (1994). 'Let's nuke the dinner: discursive practices of gender in the creation of a new cooking process', in C. Cockburn and R. Furst-Dilic (eds) *Bringing technology home*, Open University Press.

Orr Vered, K. (1998). 'Blue group boys play *Incredible Machine*, girls play hopscotch: social discourse and gendered play at the computer' in J. Sefton-Green (ed.) *Digital diversions: youth culture in the age of multimedia*, UCL Press.

Paechter, C. (2000). *Changing school subjects: power, gender and curriculum*, Open University Press.

Passey, D., Rogers, C., Machell, J., McHugh, G. and Allaway, D. (2003). *The motivational effect of ICT on pupils*, DfES Publications.

Paynter, J. (2000). 'Making progress with composing', *British Journal of Music Education*, 17(1), pp 5–31.

Pegley, K. (2000). 'Gender, voice and place: issues of negotiation in a 'technology in music program' in P. Moisala and B. Diamond (eds) *Music and gender*, University of Illinois Press.

Pendle, K. (ed.) (1991). *Women and music: a history*, Indiana University Press.

Phillips, R.J. and Pearson, A.J. (1997). 'Cognitive loads and the empowering effect of music compositional software', *Journal of Computer Assisted Learning*, 13, pp 74–84.

Piano, D. (2003). 'Resisting subjects: DIY feminism and the politics of styles in subcultural production' in D. Muggleton and R. Weinzierl (eds) *The post-subcultures reader*, Berg Publishers.

Pinch, T.P. and Bijker, W.E. (1989), 'The social construction of facts and artifacts: or how the sociology of science and the sociology of technology might benefit each other' in W.E. Bijker, T.P. Hughes and T. Pinch (eds) *The social construction of technological systems* (3rd edition), MIT Press.

Pittard, V., Bannister, P. and Dunn, P. (2003). *The big pICTure: the impact of ICT on attainment, motivation and learning*, Department for Education and Skills.

Pitts, S. (2000). *A century of change in music education: historical perspectives on contemporary practice in British secondary school music*, Ashgate Publishing.

Pitts, S. and Kwami, R. (2002). 'Raising students' performance in music composition through the use of information and communications technology (ICT): a survey of secondary schools in England', *British Journal of Music Education Research*, 19(1), pp 61–71.

Plummeridge, C. (1981). *Issues in music education*, University of London Institute of Education.

Prensky, M. (2001). 'Digital natives, digital immigrants', *On the Horizon*, 9(5), www.marcprensky.com/writing/Prensky%20-%20Digital%20Natives,%20 Digital%20Immigrants%20-%20Part1.pdf [last accessed 31 October 2010].

Prensky, M. (2009). 'H. Sapiens digital: from digital immigrants and digital natives to digital wisdom', *Innovate online*, 5(3), www.innovateonline.info/ pdf/vol5_issue3/H._Sapiens_Digital-__From_Digital_Immigrants_and_ Digital_Natives_to_Digital_Wisdom.pdf [last accessed 31 October 2010].

QCDA (2010). 'About functional skills', www.qcda.gov.uk/qualifications/ functional-skills/32.aspx [last accessed 28 August 2010].

Reay, D. (2001). 'The paradox of contemporary femininities in education: combining fluidity with fixity' in B. Francis and C. Skelton (eds) *Investigating gender: contemporary perspectives in education*, Open University Press.

Reich, N.B. (1993). 'Women as musicians: a question of class' in R. Solie (ed.) *Musicology and difference*, University of California Press.

Renold, E. and Allan, A. (2006). 'Bright and beautiful: high achieving girls, ambivalent femininities, and the feminization of success in primary school', *Discourse: Studies in the Cultural Politics of Education*, 27(4), pp 457–73.

Rogers, K. (1997). 'Resourcing music technology in secondary schools', *British Journal of Music Education*, 14, pp 129–36.

Roland Martin, J. (1994). *Changing the educational landscape: philosophy, women and curriculum*, Routledge.

Sandstrom, B. (2000). 'Women mix engineers and the power of sound' in P. Moisala and B. Diamond (eds) *Music and Gender*, University of Illinois Press.

Savage, J. (2007). 'Reconstructing music education through ICT', *Research in Education*, 78, pp 65–77.

Savage, J. and Challis, M. (2001). 'Dunwich revisited: collaborative composition and performance with new technologies', *British Journal of Music Education*, 18(2), pp 139–49.

Savage, J. and Challis, M. (2002). 'A digital arts curriculum? Practical ways forward', *Music Education Research*, 4(1), pp 7–23.

Scott, R. (1982). *Bladerunner.* Warner.

Seddon, F.A. and O'Neill, S.A (2003). 'Creative thinking processes in adolescent computer-based composition: an analysis of strategies adopted and the influence of instrumental training', *Music Education Research*, 5(2), pp 125–37.

Sefton-Green, J. (1998). *Digital diversions: youth culture in the age of multimedia*, UCL Press Ltd.

Sefton-Green, J. and Buckingham, D. (1998). 'Digital visions: children's "creative" uses of multimedia technologies' in J. Sefton-Green (ed.) *Digital diversions: youth culture in the age of multimedia*, UCL Press.

Selwyn, N. (2002). *Telling Tales on Technology: Qualitative Studies of Technology and Education*, Ashgate Publishing.

Selwyn, N. (2008). 'Developing the technological imagination: theorising the social shaping and consequences of new technologies', paper presented at the ESRC seminar series, *The Educational and Social Impact of New Technologies on Young People in Britain*. University of Oxford, 12 March.

Selwyn, N. (2011). *Schools and schooling in the digital age: a critical analysis*, Routledge.

Sheingold, K., Hawkins, J. and Char, C. (1984). 'I'm the thinkist, you're the typist: the interaction of technology and the social life of classrooms', *Journal of Social Issues*, 40(3), pp 49–61.

Shepherd, J. (1987). 'Music and male hegemony' in R. Leppert and S. McClary (eds) *Music and society: the politics of composition, performance and reception*, Cambridge University Press.

Shepherd, J. (1991). *Music as a social text*, Polity Press.

Schumacher, P. and Morahan-Martin, J. (2001). 'Gender, internet and computer attitudes and experiences', *Computers in Human Behaviour*, 17, pp 95–110.

Skelton, C. and Francis, B. (2009). *Feminism and 'the schooling scandal'*, Routledge.

Smaill, A. (2005). *Challenging gender segregation in music technology*, European Social Fund.

Smith, B. (2004). '"Boys business": an unusual northern Australian music program for boys in the middle years of schooling', *International Journal of Music Education*, 22(3), pp 230–36.

Smith, E. and Turner, S.M. (eds) (1990). *Doing it the hard way: investigations of gender and technology*, Unwin Hyman.

Sofia, Z. (1998). 'The mythic machine: gendered irrationalities and computer culture' in H. Bromley and M.W. Apple (eds) *Education/technology/power: educational computing as social practice*, State University of New York Press.

Solie, R.A. (ed.) (1993). *Musicology and difference: gender and sexuality in music scholarship*, University of California Press.

Spender, D. (1982). *Invisible women*, Writers and Readers Publishing Co-operative.

Springer, C. (1999). 'The pleasure of the interface' in J. Wolmark (ed.) *Cybersexualities: a reader on feminist theory, cyborgs and cyberspace*, Edinburgh University Press.

Squires, J. (2000). 'Fabulous feminist futures and the lure of cyberculture' in D. Bell and B.M. Kennedy (eds) *The Cybercultures Reader*, Routledge.

St John, G. (ed.) (2001). *FreeNRG: notes from the edge of the dance floor*, Common Ground Publishing.

Stensaker, B., Maassen, P., Borgan, M., Oftebro, M. and Karseth, B. (2007). 'Use, updating and integration of ICT in higher education: linking purpose, people and pedagogy', *Higher Education*, 54(3), pp 417–33.

Stepulevage, L. (2001). 'Gender/technology relations: complicating the gender binary', *Gender and Education*, 13/3, pp 325–38.

Street, J. (1992). *Politics and technology*, Macmillan Press.

Tapscott, T. (1998). *Growing up digital: rise of the net generation*, McGraw-Hill.

Taylor, T.D. (2001). *Strange sounds: music, technology and culture*, Routledge.

Théberge, P. (1997). *Any sound you can imagine: making music/consuming technology*, Wesleyan University Press.

Tjora, A.H. (2009). 'The groove in the box: a technologically mediated inspiration for electronic dance music', *Popular Music*, 28(2), pp 161–77.

Turkle, S. (1984). *The second self: computers and the human spirit*, Simon and Shuster.

Turkle, S. (1988). 'Computational reticence: why women fear the intimate machine' in C. Kramarae (ed.) *Technology and women's voices*, Routledge and Kegan Paul.

Turkle, S. (1995). *Life on the screen*, Simon and Schuster.

Turkle, S. and Papert, S. (1990). 'Epistemological pluralism: styles and voices within the computer culture', *Signs: Journal of Women in Culture and Society*, 16(1), pp 128–57.

Underwood, J., Bayuley, T., Banyard, P., Dillon, G., Farrington-Flint, L., Hayes, M., Le Geyt, G., Murphy, J. and Selwood, I. (2010). *Understanding the impact of technology: learner and school level factors*, report, British Educational Communications and Technology Agency.

Valentine, G. and Holloway, S. (2001). '"Technophobia": parents' and children's fears about information and communication technologies and the transformation of culture and society' in I. Hutchby and J. Moran-Ellis (eds) *Children, technology and culture: the impacts of technologies in children's everyday lives*, and New York: RoutledgeFalmer.

Wajcman, J. (1991). *Feminism confronts technology*, Polity Press.

Wajcman, J. (2004). *Technofeminism*, Polity Press.

Walkerdine, V. (1990), *Schoolgirl fictions*, Verso.

Walkerdine, V. (1998). *Counting girls out: girls and mathematics*, Falmer Press.

Wang, Y.S., Wu, M.C. and Wang, H.Y. (2009). 'Investigating determinants and age and gender differences in the acceptance of mobile learning', *British Journal of Educational Technology*, 40(1), pp 92–118.

Warren, S. (2003). 'Good boys are problems too!' *Pedagogy, Culture and Society*, 11(2), pp 201–213.

Watts, R. (2007). *Women in science: a social and cultural history*, Routledge.

Whistlecroft, L. (2000) 'Women in music technology in higher education in the UK', *eContact!* No. 3.3, http://cec.concordia.ca/econtact/wea2/WomenMusicTech.htm [last accessed 10 August 2004].

Whiteley, S., Bennett, A. and Hawkins, S. (2004). *Music, space and place: popular music and cultural identity*, Ashgate Publishing.

Williams, R. (1974). *Television: technology and cultural form*, Fontana.

Williams, R. (1981). *Contact: human communication and its history*, Thames and Hudson.

Williams, R. (1985). *Towards 2000*, Penguin.

Winner, L. (1977). *Autonomous technology: technics-out-of-control as a theme in political thought* (8th printing), MIT Press.

Winner, L. (1999). 'Do artifacts have politics?' in D. Mackenzie and J. Wajcman (eds) *The social shaping of technology* (2nd edition), Open University Press.

Wolmark, J. (ed.) (1999). *Cybersexualities: a reader on feminist theory, cyborgs and cyberspace'*, Edinburgh University Press.

Woolgar, S. (ed.) (2002). *Virtual society: technology, cyberbole, reality*, Oxford University Press.

Wyatt, S., Henwood, F., Miller., N and Senker, P. (2000) (eds). *Technology and in/equality: questioning the information society*, Routledge.

Yates, S.J. and Littleton, K. (2001). 'Understanding computer game cultures: a situated approach', in E. Green and A. Adam (eds), *Virtual gender: technology, consumption and identity*, Routledge.

Younger, M. (2007). 'The gender agenda in Secondary ITET in England: forgotten, misconceived or what?' *Gender and Education*, 19(3), pp 387–414.

Younger, M. and Warrington, M. (2008). 'The gender agenda in primary education in England: fifteen lost years?' *Journal of Education Policy*, 23(4), pp 429–47.

Younger, M. and Warrington, M. with Gray, J., Rudduck, J., McLellan, R., Bearne, E., Kershner, R. and Bricheno, P. (2005). *Raising boys' achievement*, Research Report No. 636, Department for Education and Skills.

Index